MAYNIAC

THE BIOGRAPHY OF
CONOR MAYNARD

MAYNIAC

THE BIOGRAPHY OF
CONOR MAYNARD

MARTIN HOWDEN

JOHN BLAKE

Published by John Blake Publishing Ltd,
3 Bramber Court, 2 Bramber Road,
London W14 9PB, England

www.johnblakepublishing.co.uk

www.facebook.com/Johnblakepub   facebook
twitter.com/johnblakepub   twitter

First published in paperback in 2013

ISBN: 978 1 78219 455 2

British Library Cataloguing-in-Publication Data:

A catalogue record for this book is available from the British Library.

Design by www.envydesign.co.uk

Printed and bound in Great Britain by CPI Group (UK) Ltd

1 3 5 7 9 10 8 6 4 2

CONTENTS

CHAPTER ONE

BRIGHTON BOY

Described by music star Pharrell Williams as the 'kid who will change the face of pop music', Conor Paul Maynard has carried the weight of others' expectations on his slight shoulders ever since he first sung in front of a makeshift microphone in his bedroom and uploaded the subsequent result onto YouTube. Luckily, the young singer has shown that he is more than able to meet the lofty expectations placed upon him.

It all began after a chance encounter on the streets of his beloved hometown of Brighton. The popular young teen was messing about and having fun with his friends. Always the performer, Conor couldn't resist showing off and decided to sing in front of them.

He explained to the *Telegraph* in a 2011 interview: 'There was this one day, four years ago, when I was walking down the road after school, and I was singing to myself and messing about with my friends. An older girl from school turned around and said, "Boy, you can sing!"'

His impromptu rendition of Usher and R. Kelly's 'Same Girl' caused such a ruckus that the girl, impressed by his delicate and soulful voice, turned around open-mouthed and exclaimed: 'Wow, do that again!' Laughing it off, Conor thanked her for the compliments and ego-boosting moment before continuing on his merry way. But she had no desire to end it there. The next day she cornered him at school and forced him to sing in front of her pals. As word got round, Conor was soon wheeled out in front of more school friends, mostly female, and forced to sing on the spot.

It became such a playground ritual that he soon began to grow in confidence. However, Conor soon tired of his spare time being taken up with singing in front of girls and decided to come up with an alternative way to perform. Bolstered by the popularity of his musical ability, it made sense to transform his small bedroom into a makeshift studio and sing some covers for friends. Conor immersed himself in music technology and the videos of his favourite stars like Chris Brown and Ne-Yo, ensuring that his YouTube uploads, thanks to his singing and editing ability, were far ahead of the usual amateur efforts that regularly clog up the website. Before he knew it, those videos were attracting a far bigger audience than his school pals in Brighton. He was fast becoming a social networking and YouTube phenomenon with more than 90 million combined YouTube views and over a million followers on Twitter.

His success is staggering when you realise he was just a normal boy from a working-class family, living in Brighton. In the current climate, when more and more 'pop stars' are created from reality TV and manufactured to within an inch of their lives, this gifted young singer was a breath of fresh air, with success coming thanks to hard work combined with talent.

His amazing rise to stardom is an incredible journey, and it all began on 21 November 1992 when he was welcomed into the world by his parents, Helen and Gary. Conor also has a younger brother called Jack, and a little sister called Anna.

He was born and grew up in Brighton until he was eventually forced to move at the age of 18, following his success. It's a place that will always be home to him, despite the inevitable trappings that come with being a pop superstar. Memories of growing up in Brighton live with him and he has regularly stated in interviews that he misses his hometown.

Brighton is a major city on the south coast of Great Britain. During the 18th century it emerged as a popular health resort destination, later attracting thousands of day-trippers from nearby London following the introduction of The London & Brighton Railway in 1841, prompting the oft-attributed phrase: 'London-by-the-sea'. The subsequent growth saw major attractions being built during the Victorian era, including the Grand Hotel and the Palace Pier.

Brighton is now famous for its thriving seafront, filled with bars, restaurants and nightclubs between the piers. Every weekend, the area is buzzing with large party groups, many of them on stag and hen celebrations. Those who grow up in Brighton soon get used to mingling with the weekend trade. The mild atmosphere of the weekday seafront, filled with locals and easy-going tourists strolling along the pebbled beach and eating out at the many seafood restaurants, is hijacked at weekends by drunken brides-to-be wearing L plates and young men, their eyes glazed, hanging limply onto each other as they stumble their way into another neon-lit bar with the promise of cheap alcohol scrawled on chalkboards.

Once the weekend is over, normality returns to the popular seafront and the locals go back to their regular routine. Despite its reputation for being a party city, Brighton also has an enormous amount of culture. Away from the heady drunken atmosphere lies the North Laine. Comprising 300 shops, over 20 pubs and several theatres and museums, the area is famous for its independent shops and lively, cultured atmosphere. It is adjacent to the Royal Pavilion, and was once seen as a slum area. Now it's best known for being the bohemian hub and cultural heartbeat of Brighton.

Growing up, Conor was a regular on North Laine and it's here that he bought his first microphone in one of the trendy music stores, following the success of his early YouTube videos. He told *ilikemusic.com*: 'Brighton was definitely an inspirational place to grow up, though. There were a lot of musicians coming out of there, like Rizzle Kicks. I dunno what it is about it, but it's a cool place to be. A lot of people see it as London-by-the-sea.'

Conor's mother was an office worker, his dad was a builder, and his childhood was one filled with love and affection. The family would spend many of their summer holidays staying in caravan parks across the country. However, he was misquoted in a 2012 interview when it was claimed that they spent all their holidays at caravan parks simply because they were poor.

Conor explained: 'I remember one newspaper said, apparently I said that my family are really deprived and really poor, and we used to go on caravan holidays all the time and that's all we could afford. No! That's isn't what I said! I told them that it was amazing that I got to record around the world because when I was younger, my mum used to love to go on caravan holidays. She likes to stay in the UK, so she loved different caravan park holidays. We weren't poor and deprived – that's just what she loved doing because that's what she used to do when she was younger, and they took that and turned it into the fact that I was really poor and all this kind of shit and I was like, "No, that's not true."'

In fact, he did enjoy foreign travels growing up. When asked what his best childhood memory was, he told *The Yorker*: 'The first time I went to America, we went to Florida – to Disneyland and Bush Gardens. I also got the first tan of my life, which is always good.'

Conor is extremely close to his brother, whom he affectionately dubs 'Jacky-pops' in interviews. Of their childhood, Jack said in an interview: 'We never really argued at all; we got on really well. He would always sing. Always. We both listened to the same music – RnB and hip-hop. We had a little rock phase when we were younger.'

In the kitchen of the family home there is a notice board covered with leaflets and old family photos. Several of these photos feature the two boys together, including a picture of them dressed up as chefs, and one where they are enjoying themselves on the Isle of Wight. Beside it, another photo has the brothers re-enacting the same image a few years later.

Jack has taken over the room where Conor completed his famous recordings but his elder sibling doesn't seem to care that the room that formed his childhood, with the piano in the corner and the balcony overlooking the garden below – used in early videos to give it more of a superstar look – now belongs to his brother.

Jack looks up to Conor. Little wonder, really, as he is currently soaking up the perks of having a famous brother. Not only does he now have the big room after Conor moved to London (fans found out where he lived and began to leave

Post-it notes on the door of his home after he became famous), but he has also appeared in one of his brother's music videos. He has also become a magnet for short-sighted paparazzo: on leaving nightclubs in Brighton, Jack has been photographed by celebrity snappers in the mistaken belief that he is his big brother. Luckily, he sees the funny side of it and just laughs off the attention.

Conor revealed in an interview: 'My brother actually got papped outside a club because they thought it was me. He was standing there just absolutely laughing his head off and the paparazzi guy just looked so confused. We'll see if fame corrupts him!'

On moving to London, Conor said: 'I do like living here. If you want to do what I want to do and be in the music industry, it's the place to be. All the labels are here, all the studios are here. It's much easier being in London, but I do miss Brighton quite a lot sometimes, especially some of the people back there.'

With Conor leaving home, for Jack there was another treat in store.

Conor explained to the *Telegraph*: 'When I was younger, playing video games was my life; when I moved away from Brighton, I promised I'd leave my younger brother my Xbox, so now in my flat, I just have a PS3. I love games – I will get them the day they come out. I'm a real geek.' In fact, when asked if 2012 was the best year of his life, he remarked: 'I would say so. Apart from 2007, when I got a PlayStation 2 for Christmas. There's a battle there, but yeah, it's definitely been a big year!'

Growing up, the youngsters were made to feel very special by their parents and encouraged to believe in themselves and their abilities. In Conor's case, early on it became apparent that he loved music. His mother revealed in a BBC Radio 1 interview: 'He liked music from a really young age. He picked up songs straight away. I can remember when Conor was a really small baby, in his bouncy chair hanging off the doorframe, and we used to put on Gabrielle's "Dreams" and he would bounce up and down to that for hours on end. He liked to entertain people from a very, very young age. Even now, if he pops home, he'll be bursting into song. He was always singing, but he didn't think he was anything special.'

When it became clear that his ambitions were focused on performing, his mother did all she could to nurture his talent, encouraging him to learn musical instruments as a young child and take up acting when he grew a bit older. Conor told the

Telegraph: 'When I was young my mum noticed I loved performing – I used to burst into song in the middle of the doctor's waiting-room – and she enrolled me in a drama school on Saturdays.'

She didn't always listen to what her son wanted, though.

Conor added: 'When I was eight, I wanted to change my name to Leo because I loved lions so much. Luckily, my mum just laughed at me.'

He also learnt piano, telling the newspaper: 'I had piano lessons when I was younger, but I quit because I didn't want to sit and learn the scales. I just went on the internet and used tutorials to teach myself how to play songs on my keyboard. I can't read music, but I'm glad I know how to play because it means I can have more input in my songs.'

His parents are understandably proud of their son. In the family home, close to the childhood portraits that hang on the living room wall, is a giant poster of Conor's debut single, 'Can't Say No'.

Conor said on 'Postcodes', a YouTube video he created about his life: 'My mother is very proud of my achievements so far. It's kind of crazy to look at, seeing as I started this whole thing in my house. It's really special to me [coming home] as I now live in London. It's a little escape from the craziness that I do with my music.'

He added: 'I'm from Brighton, which is probably best known for its beach. The beach holds a lot of memories for me, with my friends coming here on sunny days. It was this town [where] I did my first cover; I had my first million views. It all happened in Brighton – I never lived anywhere else. A lot of amazing things have happened that have contributed to my story and where I am now.'

Conor is incredibly close to his parents, dubbing them his 'heroes' in an interview.

It's clear that his father is responsible for his son's performing bug. While he has worked in the building trade for many years, Gary Maynard was once an actor and appeared in several West End productions. Also, his granddad used to sing in jazz clubs, emulating Rat-Pack icons such as Frank Sinatra and Dean Martin.

Conor said: 'My dad, Gary – he's a builder now, but he used to be an actor on the West End stage. My granddad is another hero. He used to sing Rat-Pack-style music in jazz clubs. They both inspired me to get up and perform.'

Both his parents were heavily into music, and, growing up, Conor was immersed in the sound of rhythm and blues. He told *Idolator*: 'When I was really young, my parents listened to people like Michael Jackson, Stevie Wonder – a lot of R&B-pop acts. And then as I got into the early teens – 13 and 14 – I listened to Green Day and Good Charlotte. As I got older, in terms of mid-teens, that's when the real R&B started to come in. So I was listening to a lot of Usher, Mario, Justin Timberlake, Ne-Yo, Brandy. For me, R&B was definitely the more influential music I used to listen to. I was so inspired by the way they would sing, kind of the technical thing they would do with their voice. It made me figure out I wanted to be able to sing like that.'

He told *Glamour* magazine: 'From a really young age, I couldn't really talk properly yet, and I just used to say the numbers of what track I knew was on the CD, and they had to put that one on. And also, I couldn't say music so I used to say "sic" and they knew that when I said "sic on", I wanted [them] to put the music on. But my aunty who used to babysit me had no idea what it meant. She thought I was going to throw up, like, "I'm going to be sick!" So my mum used to have to come and pick me up.'

Talking more about his biggest icon, Michael Jackson, Conor remarked: 'I've never seen a performer that's greater than him. I definitely still consider him one of the all-time greatest performers. He had it all: he had the voice that was incredible, his musical style was amazing; he was very professional about everything that he did. I heard that before he recorded a demo, hc would warm up his voice for an hour. Everything he did was very on point and clever. He's definitely an artist that I look up to.'

Like any young boy, even with the impressive musical influences inherited from his parents, there was still some embarrassing music in Conor's collection. He admitted: 'Me and my friends were the Blue of Brighton and Hove. I think I was Lee Ryan, actually – that was the person I would be. We loved Blue and we would sing all of their songs. We made a whole S Club Juniors [now known as S Club 8] as well.'

He added to the *Guardian*: 'I was about nine. At break time, me and three of my friends would pretend we were Blue. I was Lee Ryan. We tried to do the dancing, but some of us weren't into it. I was a massive fan but after the album *Guilty*, I moved on.'

He also admitted: 'This is embarrassing. When I was eight, me and my brother and our next-door neighbour would take the CD player into our back garden. We'd put the Pokémon theme tune on repeat, and get on our bikes and ride round and round and round. The garden wasn't even that big. We were like, "Oh my goodness, we're going to catch a Pokémon!" "Play it more than 30 times."'

In between hours devoted to video games, Conor was obsessed with Pokémon, particularly collecting cards of the characters from the hit animated series. He revealed: 'The shiny Charizard card was my ultimate goal when I was younger. My next door neighbour's brother told us he had one and that he'd only give it to us if we beat him at a game of tennis so me, my brother and my neighbour trained for tennis every day and played his brother every day. We finally beat him and then he told us he didn't have it. It was literally one of the worst days ever.'

Another guilty pleasure is the *High School Musical* soundtrack on his iPod.

When asked what he remembered about being 12, Conor said: 'If I think back to then, all I remember is being in my garden with my brother and my friends. We had a trampoline, so I was always on the trampoline, and playing different games. When I was 12, I was probably the shortest one among my friends, but I did have a growth spurt and then I became one of the tall kids. But then I stayed there and everyone else started growing, so then I became one of the short kids again. I kind of wore very baggy clothes – I was going through the skater phase. I had all my baggy jeans on and big clunky shoes.'

'I was pretty loud,' he added. 'I was pretty much the class joker – I tried to pay attention.'

He was educated at Cardinal Newman Catholic School in Hove – a mixed comprehensive. The official website for the school states: 'When students gain a place at Cardinal Newman Catholic School they will be welcomed into a community that prides itself on its care for each individual. Our school mission statement celebrates the uniqueness of each person. We recognise the personal and academic differences within our student body and it is our goal to offer the appropriate level of support and challenge that ensures individual growth and success.

'Parents entrust their children to us and it is our task to join in a partnership with the home to raise every child in a secure environment built on Christian principles that prepare every student for the world they will meet as adults. Sound discipline, care, support and academic challenge are our guidelines and we are confident that your child will benefit from her/his time at Cardinal Newman Catholic School. All students are encouraged to contribute towards our further growth.'

He told CBBC about his schooldays: 'I used to get lost all the time, and had to pull on some big kid's jumper: "Can you tell me where the office is?", and he would lead me to a field. I'd be standing in the field, thinking, "I don't think this is the office"

'You had to stand up in front of the class and give presentations and stuff. I started to develop this thing where I would stand there and sway. I couldn't stand still, so that was kind of embarrassing.'

At school, Conor was nicknamed Coco Pop, due to a mole under his eye that is similar to the famous chocolate cereal. Although he wasn't the most popular kid in the school, he was well liked and hovered around the social status that saw him sitting close to the end of the bus during coach trips without fear of being intimidated by the cooler kids.

His best friend Alex recalled in an interview with BBC's Radio 1: 'Conor's personality has always been about being fun. On our first ever lesson he said something that made me laugh, I said something that made him laugh. From there on our sense of humour was exactly the same. You know that feeling with your best friend when you laugh at things no one else will do? We used to always muck about. We had science and maths together, and we'd be sitting there and we'd be beatboxing. I remember him teaching me, and we'd be beatboxing "Billie Jean" [Michael Jackson] or something like that. From there he just started singing, and every single lesson he'd be singing. He would get progressively better every day. Even when I was writing, he would just be singing. It's weird because that would probably be every girl's dream just to hear him singing right next to you for an hour. But for me I was like, "Shut up, that's really annoying now!"'

In between wanting to be the centre of attention, Conor was a keen reader, with J. K. Rowling's hugely successful series about teen wizard Harry Potter a particular favourite. He explained: 'I always used to get really into a lot of different books growing up. Obviously, I read all the Harry Potters. I remember I used to get really tied into the whole story when I was reading it. It's almost the same as music, where you can interpret it in your own way. Like when you read a book, you can imagine the characters in your own way, what they look like, what their personalities are, and you can interpret it in your own way. It's like a song. When you're listening to music, one song can have a million different meanings to all different people. You can fit your own situations into it. That was also my favourite part about books: that you could interpret [them] in your own way. You could fill out your part of the story in your own imagination.

'I used to love *A Series of Unfortunate Events*, those books. I used to absolutely love those books. I remember I read all 13 of them twice. Yeah, I was a big fan of those books when I was growing up, so I would definitely recommend them. They're very clever.'

Around this time Conor's musical taste was ever growing, and he later observed: 'Probably my favourite artist when I was in that transition from primary school to secondary school was Eminem. I was such a big fan of him. Obviously, there was "Toy Soldiers", which came out around then. That was probably one of my favourites. I got my piano teacher to listen to Eminem. She was like, 80-something. She'd be sitting in the house listening to it and figuring out the piano parts so she could teach me my next lesson. Eminem was quite influential to me – I never really listened to rap before him. It brought me into rap, and with the kind of music I do now, it kind of has a link to that.'

Despite coming from Brighton, Conor is in fact a Manchester United fan and he grew up supporting the famous team. When asked what his favourite colour was, he answered: 'Red, I supported Manchester United when I was little.'

A sporty kid, he enjoyed football and badminton: 'When I was in school, obviously football was something I played a lot. I used to love badminton, though. It may be a random one, but it was so much fun. It's not easy. Obviously, it's not hard to play, but to master it is hard. But when it's just hitting a feather, it's like, "I can't get hurt, I'm so happy". Because with a football it will hit you in the face and you'll be like, "Oh, that really hurts!" With a shuttlecock it's just all a bit carefree.'

Conor showed his kind-hearted side after raising money to help those in need following the 2004 Indian Ocean earthquake and tsunami, which killed over 200,000 people. He told CBBC: 'The big news story when I was 12 was the tsunami hitting Thailand on Boxing Day. I saw lots of pictures and different videos of it – it was one of the most craziest things I have ever seen. I never knew that waves could be that towering and big; that will probably never leave my head. I remember my school did a fundraiser for it. We just did a whole bunch of things to raise money.'

While he was to be a regular in the music charts, it wasn't just singing that Conor was interested in during those early days. From the age of seven he had been desperate to be an actor and he would attend drama school every Saturday to indulge his then main passion. He said: 'I went to K-BIS Theatre School part-time at weekends. I only did singing because all my friends who went there did it. Acting was my main focus.'

The school's website states: 'Brighton's Premier Performing Arts School opened in 1998 and has since been in business as a national and internationally successful Full-Time/Part-Time Academic Performing Arts School providing a balanced vocational and academic education for boys and girls aged between three and 18+'.

Nine-year-old Conor took to the stage as a young Michael for the Theatre Royal Brighton's performance of *Peter Pan* and his daredevil heroics saw him flying on stage on a harness.

He would study at the K-BIS Theatre School for 10 years. Although this was a part-time course, Conor took it seriously and attended both weekend and weekday classes. Showcasing his determination and willingness to learn, he would listen intently in a bid to make it as an actor.

In an interview for this book, Principal Marcia

King recalled: 'Conor was a part-time student at K-BIS Theatre School for 10 years. He studied Drama, Singing and Musical Theatre. He took part in many productions as an actor/singer/dancer. He appeared professionally in the TV series *Dream Team* as the younger self of another K-BIS success, Rob Kazinsky – from *EastEnders* and now making films in Hollywood – he attended not only on Saturdays but during the week. He took part in several Drama and Musical Theatre examinations as part of a large cast, which gained him many Distinctions and as a Solo candidate at A-level he gained as an actor over 90 marks and [a] High Distinction.'

She added: 'He has a wonderful ability to listen and take direction from our professional directors, choreographers and musical directors, and deserves every bit of success as he understands that you have to work hard, be pleasant to everyone and to deliver the goods! He visits us from time to time and our younger students seem to scream or become utterly tongue-tied when they meet him! His sister is still a student at K-BIS.'

As Marcia stated, Conor also appeared on the Sky 1 football soap, *The Dream Team*. The long-running Sky 1 (and later Sky 3) series followed the adventures of the fictional football team Harchester United, and ran from 1997 to 2007.

This sporting drama focused on the on- and off-field activities of its players and the fans. On the testimonial section of the website for K-BIS Theatre School, Conor is quoted as saying: 'In the 10 years I spent at K-BIS I gained confidence and techniques to follow my dream to become a performer.'

Rob Kazinsky also credits his success to K-BIS. On the webpage he states: 'To be a professional doesn't mean just to be paid, it means to be on time, it means to know your lines, it means to behave with a certain demeanour and observance of a command structure, to understand that there's a hierarchy, to know how a production is put together and to always give your best, your utmost, to do yourself, the character and the production the service, you, they and it deserve. I knew nothing the first day I entered K-BIS, though of course I thought I did, and over the time that I worked with Marcia and the other teachers at K-BIS they stripped me of my arrogance (to a point!) and rebuilt me, moulded me and helped focus me in the direction I had always wanted to pull. Being a true professional is rare even in the higher echelons of the industry and directors and producers will always want to work with somebody worth working with.'

He went on: 'I was always a wayward child and

having an environment like K-BIS, surrounded by like-minded people, allowed me to be who I needed to be to succeed, supported by my friends and teachers, some of whom I wouldn't have been able to survive as a person without.'

Conor added to Capital FM: 'It's funny because music wasn't really my first kind of interest, it was actually acting. I went to a theatre school part-time on Saturdays when I was younger but I only really sung because everyone who also went would do drama, singing and dancing. So because everybody did both I didn't want to be left out so I did the singing and dancing too, but drama and acting was kind of the main thing for me when I was younger. I was actually in *Dream Team* on Sky 1 when I was 13. I still think to this day it would kind of be a dream of mine to do the whole Justin Timberlake singing-to-acting thing, that would be really cool.'

Despite spending many years honing his skills as an actor and impressing his drama teachers with his skills, willingness to learn and effort, Conor began to realise that another passion was forming in his life. It soon became clear that while he was born to be a performer, for him it wasn't about being in front of the camera but instead being in the recording booth.

He told *Just Youth*: 'I always sang when I was younger – I think it was when I was around 15 when my voice kind of broke and I started singing more. People started saying I had quite a unique voice so I carried on singing after that. So I think the main time was just after school when I was walking down a road and I was singing "Same Girl" by Usher and R. Kelly to my friends and this girl a few passes ahead turned round and shouted "You can sing!" And then they came up to me and made me sing for everyone at school the next day, and everyone was like, really "Oh, wow!" so that was really the moment when I remember thinking maybe I should do something with this.'

The young Conor always had a natural talent when it came to singing, as his mother revealed: 'When he was about 11 he began to realise he would get picked if there was any solo parts. He would often be picked out for those. And when he left primary school, the deputy head was getting married and she wanted the school choir to sing at her wedding, and Conor was picked to do one of the solos. I think at that point he was beginning to notice that maybe he had a good voice.'

In July 2012, Conor recalled: 'I think when I started to listen to my own thing, it was very RnB-related – a lot of Usher, Justin Timberlake. Before then, I enjoyed performing quite a lot, but really, the main part of performing that I loved was acting. That was my main passion until about the age of 15, so before then I listened to music but it wasn't really [my thing]. I used to just listen to random things, and that was it. And after the age of 15, I started to really get into things. Right now, it's a lot of hip-hop, like Drake, Jay-Z, Kanye West, so it's changed as I've grown up.'

Many pop-star wannabes try their luck on reality TV shows such as X Factor. This, however, was never an option for Conor, who had already witnessed how ruthless the series could be when it came to one of his friends. He said: 'I never really got the chance to think about it. I was still in college when the whole YouTube thing blew up; I didn't realise that it was going to go that crazy and I had to leave college early to pursue the music career. It was mad. I mean, Ne-Yo himself saw one of my covers and tried to sign me and that created this buzz of like "Who is this kid that Ne-Yo wants to take off to America and sign?" It was like a whirlwind in the way it started; I was signed very quickly. So I never really got the chance to think about how else I would have really done it. But I know that I was always planning to do it more just like sending off demos and music to labels. I had a friend who was just incredible but she never got through the first round of *X Factor* and so I kind of think: Well, I don't know what they're looking for. She had the most insane voice.'

Despite not wanting to be on the show, *The X Factor* was a huge thing for Conor and his pals when the series first started. He revealed: 'I remember the winner, Steve Brookstein. I think I was rooting for him, so I was happy for that. It was the first one, so everyone was talking about it. It was the big talking point at school so if you missed it, you were out of the loop for a week – you had to wait till next week to have friends again.'

He was just a normal boy, with dreams shared by many adolescents hoping to seize their share of the limelight, and although he longed to become famous, he was also careful to enjoy his time away from his performing aspirations.

Conor used to hang around Churchill Square shopping centre in Brighton with his friends and despite his glitzy lifestyle they still form part of his life. It seems important for him to hang onto the friendships he had before he became famous in a bid to stay grounded. Soon after his early success, he would end up playing an acoustic gig at a nearby HMV store on Churchill Square – prompting a mob of screaming fans to grab at him.

'It was literally insane,' he said. 'I had no idea that people were going to turn out like that – it was really cool to see. It made me so excited just thinking that I'm about to do it in my hometown. I used to go to Churchill Square all the time, so it's going to be really weird seeing that in a place I know so well.'

He now lives in London and admitted to *ilikemusic.com*: 'I did leave at quite a good time – when I went off, everyone else went off to uni anyway. So it's not like everyone's back in Brighton having a party without me.'

Despite the lavish lifestyle, he will always be a Brighton boy, revealing: 'I was born and bred in Hove (and went to Cardinal Newman School), and it's definitely home for me. But I live in London now – but for me my family still live in Brighton. I try and go back as much as possible, see my family and my friends.'

Of fame, he said: 'I never get to go home anymore – I'm so busy that I don't get back to Brighton as much as I used to. I went down recently and my mum still made me take out the recycling.'

And he's delighted that he gets the same

treatment from his friends, revealing: 'They think it's crazy! Sometimes I get Facebook posts saying "It's so weird hearing you on the radio" or "I just saw your music on the TV!" At the moment it's number one on 4Music and Fresh on The Box, so people are like, "What! You're on it *and* you're number one?" I have to point out that it isn't the actual chart! But my closest friends keep me very grounded. They still see me as Conor the idiot, not Conor the singer.'

He added: 'They see me as the kid they've known for years, and they take every chance to rinse me and take the piss out of me, 'cos they're my mates and that's what we do to each other! I was taught by my vocal coach a long time ago that you need to be able to turn it off when you step off the stage. When you're on the stage you've got to be that big showman, but when you're off stage with your friends, you've got to go back to being who you were before.'

In another interview, he continued on the same theme: 'I'm lucky though because my family and friends still treat me like the same idiot I was before all this! They are helping me keep my feet on the ground throughout all this hype.'

But there is also a downside to fame, with Conor telling *Showbiz 411*: 'Funnily enough, I always wanted to make a point of not changing my number because I wanted to see who would crawl out of the woodwork and say "Hey, remember me? I love you!" And I'd be like, "I don't remember your name." But sometimes you have the odd person [on Facebook] saying, "We were best friends, remember" – it's just funny.'

While his fame continues to grow and his passport bears the stamps of more and more glamorous and exotic locations, it's still the pebbled beach with the riotous weekend atmosphere that has a hold on him: 'It was a cool place to grow up. There's the beach, the city as well as a lot of farmland going on. I suppose the versatility emulated onto my music as well – I've got quite versatile influences. Growing up, I used to listen to people like Michael Jackson, Stevie Wonder, then I went through a very RnB stage with like, Usher, Mario, Justin Timberlake and I also listen to people like Green Day and Good Charlotte as well, and now I listen to a lot of rap. They're really supportive to young musicians – they've got Brighton's music group and there's a lot of talent shows and open mic nights.'

CHAPTER TWO

CAUGHT ON THE WEB

Every pop star has one – that single moment, the one time they can trace back to the definitive moment when their path to a life in music was set in front of them.

In Conor's case, it was that moment when a female school friend was compelled to tell him that he could sing. He recalled: 'I knew her quite well, but she didn't know I could sing. She would have been brutally honest if I couldn't sing. She would have been like, "Don't do that again"'. Following that encounter, it wasn't long before he decided to record his own versions of other people's songs on

YouTube. Tired of having to sing in front of female friends at school and college, he decided to post his videos on the social networking site.

He explained to the *Telegraph* that it was 'mainly so I'd get to eat my lunch at school rather than having to sing all through my break.'

The girl who would go on to become famous for her impromptu reaction was Ebony Galea, who was just walking home from school when she heard her pal singing a song. She would go on to become a catalyst for Conor's success.

While Conor has said in previous interviews that he was singing with his friends, Ebony remembers it differently. She told this author: 'From what I remember he was at a bus stop by himself. I was like, "Wow, Conor you can sing!" It was really delicate, but it was clear he had talent. He used to sing to me all the time but he just didn't have the confidence. I made him sing in front of the girls – they loved him.

'No one really knew too much about his success. The boys didn't take him seriously; it was more for the girls. I used to go home and watch him on YouTube, and my brother would be like, "Who's that? What are you watching?"'

Talking about how she met him, she continued: 'We're the same age, I used to be in his English class. We used to be very close and always together.

Whenever he wasn't there with me people would ask, "Where's Conor, is he ill?" I first met him at IT class, I think. He used to sit next to me and he always made me smile and laugh. He was pretty popular. He used to always make me laugh.'

She added: 'He used to send me a YouTube cover every time he did one and we still speak to each other now.'

In another interview she said: 'It spiralled from me telling him he could sing. I got his confidence up so he could sing to other people. I used to tell him to go on *X Factor* and he wouldn't. If he was going to do it, he was wanting to do it on his own.'

Conor said: 'It just started going around school that I could sing, and no one really knew. And then yeah, it suddenly became widespread knowledge that I could sing. There weren't really many guy singers who could sing in my year. I plucked up the courage to sing in school – I think it was the last day of Year 11 when I finished school. I sung "Chasing Cars" by Snow Patrol, and it was crazy, everyone got mad on stage.'

He added to *Sonic Nation*: 'When word got around that I could sing, I got asked almost every day to sing for them, mainly girls. It was good, though, as it mainly urged me to go "Maybe I should do something with this"'.

While he knew what the next step would be, he wanted to make sure that he understood as much as possible about uploading videos on to the internet. He had signed up to YouTube in 2006, but it wasn't until two years later that he uploaded his very first video. It was a cover version of Lee Carr's ballad 'Breathe', released on 1 December 2008. Accompanying the track was the message: 'I recorded this in my room sooo the quality may not be amazing lol'. Although he would later film his videos, he uploaded 'Breathe' with just an arty black and white photo of himself.

His brother Jack recalled: 'I remember going into his room and there was these two microphones taped together and he was trying to sing into that. I just laughed at him and told him he was an idiot. I just thought he was embarrassing himself.'

Conor told *FirstNews*: 'My first cover song was recorded with a SingStar microphone, which I unplugged from the PlayStation and plugged into my computer. After that, I started to get more into it. I got a proper microphone and camera and started doing more covers filmed in my room.'

His online debut was low key, and he admitted to BBC Radio 1's Nick Grimshaw: 'The earlier ones I did were awful. I loved "Breathe" by Lee Carr. He's a really unknown artist I found randomly going through music online. And I look back at it now and it was so bad. I didn't know how to record it, didn't know how to put any effects on it or anything; it was just really raw. It was my first ever cover, it was the first thing I ever recorded. It just doesn't sound good. Hope the fans will have mercy when they first hear it. I was a beginner back then when I didn't really know what I was doing.'

At a Google Q and A, he said: 'My first one [video] was so bad. There's just a picture of me and I look awful. My head is so round and I just look awful – like I'm an Employee of the Month. It's just one of these things, though. You learn with each one and you grow.'

Eight days later, he released his second effort, a soulful cover of Daniel D's "The Truth". This was another romantic ballad, and it was clear that he was positioning himself as a crooner for the ladies. Like 'Breathe', the image accompanying the track was a moody portrait. This time it was in colour, with a contemplative Conor hunched near the microphone and staring off into the distance.

Two days on from this he released another cover, but this time he accompanied it with a personal message: 'me singing a cover of Usher's "Something Special" for my love :) x x x'. He also did a cover of Beyoncé's 'If I Were A Boy'. This time it was different, with his sister Anna adorably duetting with him.

He subsequently uploaded 'Breathe' again on 15 February 2010 and dedicated the track to his then girlfriend, Marisha D'Arcy. Conor wrote: 'Thought I would have another go at Lee Carr's "Breathe" for Valentine's Day for the one I love :) Although this is for her I hope anyone who felt they didn't have a special Valentines, or who had an amazing one, can still enjoy this song!!! :) Happy Belated Valentines!!!' Because it was the cheapest software he could find and it was also easy to use, he spent £40 on the home recording program Mixcraft and used karaoke backing tracks, too.

Later, when asked if it was strange for him to have complete strangers seeing his bedroom, he replied: 'Yes, it is! Especially since it is so messy. My room is an absolute dump and my mum wasn't so happy that people were seeing it. I used to do videos, some of which had a million views, and my mum would get really angry with me because I'd uploaded it as you can see dirty laundry and my bed wasn't made. She didn't like them because she said her house looks like a mess!'

His mother Helen revealed: 'He said definitely he was going to take music technology. At that point, I said to him, "Is that because you want to work in the music industry?" He said, "No, just because it will help me upload my music videos on to YouTube. I'll know more about the equipment I'm using." I was like, "For goodness' sake, you need a proper career. Forget YouTube!"'

Luckily, Conor didn't listen to his mother. With primitive technology at hand, he was taking his first tentative steps into the unknown. The path would soon be paved with musical riches, but at that precise moment he had no real idea what was going to happen next. He was hedging his bets on his makeshift studio, which featured the two SingStar microphones sellotaped together.

Conor said: 'They didn't really blow up after a year of it, when I was in college. I didn't really do videos then, either – I would record a cover and I would just have a picture of me. It didn't really draw many people in to watch it. And through trial and error I began to know a bit more about recording. I got a better microphone and I got a better set-up.'

He added to the *Yorker*: 'I think for me when I first started, it was just something I enjoyed doing as a hobby. I didn't really think in my head what it would become. I would come home from college and sit in my room and think of a song to do a cover of, and that's what made it even more amazingly exciting when it did happen, because it wasn't something I saw coming. When it all blew up and I got all these crazy reviews and people contacting me to ask to work with me it was amazing.'

The first few attempts would see around 30 or 40 views over the week; one week in particular saw two comments posted by his mum, without realising that she had posted the same one twice.

'I was happy with a few hundred views a month and my nan commenting and saying she liked it,' said Conor.

Homework would be put to one side as he came home from college to work on his covers instead, with his dad banging on the ceiling, telling him to keep the noise down.

Conor recalled: 'When I first started it was very unknown tracks, random songs off people's albums, like a track off Mario's album, an Usher track, songs that people didn't really know and then I did "Signed, Sealed, Delivered" by Stevie Wonder and some other older songs. I started getting millions of hits on YouTube. It was just a track and a picture; after a while I put up videos with me performing the song, and that's when it really started to kick off.'

Conor told the *Edge*: 'I didn't know anyone who had a studio – I didn't know anyone who recorded anything – so for me, I had to learn it all by myself. I started using my webcam, it was crap, but that was just how I started and then I started to go online and learnt about microphones, and when birthdays or Christmas came along, I would get the stuff that I wanted.'

Playing a white piano, he would play several heartfelt songs, while his mother would record later songs on a small camera.

His first success came following collaboration with another Brightonian, Beckie Eaves.

'We had about 10,000 views,' he said. 'We had got famous in Brighton; people in Brighton started to know the songs.'

Uploading songs became a regular occurrence and he was soon releasing covers at an increasing rate, joined in his singing ventures by Anthony 'Anth' Melo – an American rapper who hails from Virginia.

Conor said of their unlikely team-up: 'It was the power of the internet. Anth found a video I made ages ago [on YouTube], back when I was first doing my covers. It was recorded with quite a good quality microphone. He contacted me about doing a collaboration so I checked out his stuff, thought it was really cool. I said, "Definitely let's do it." We came up with a couple of ideas and ended up doing a cover of "OMG" [(Oh My Gosh)] by Usher. We recorded our parts, sent them to each other and it was all through the internet – never met at this point, put it together through Skype and emails. When we uploaded it, it blew up, so obviously we did more and more covers.'

He added to the *Telegraph*: 'Then he suggested we record a video of ourselves singing it. I used my mum's camcorder, and we put it up and a few weeks later it had 70,000 views. I thought, we've made it!'

Anth told this author: 'The first video I ever saw of Conor was his cover of Sean Kingston and Justin Bieber's "Eenie Meenie". There was no video, just a picture. I remember it was in the related videos and I clicked it on accident. I let it play in the background and I remember hearing his voice thinking, "Whoa, who's this singing?" So I went back to the video and found out it was by some guy named Conor Maynard. I checked out the rest of his videos and couldn't believe how amazing his voice was, and the tone of his voice as well – it was just so different than any other singer out there. There were thousands and thousands of singers on YouTube, and Conor was the only one who ever actually stood out to me. I must've watched every single one of his videos before messaging him for the very first time.'

Although Anth wasn't looking for a partner, he became convinced that there was something unique about him: 'I've always been and wanted to be a solo artist so when I came across Conor for the first time, partnering up together the way we did was definitely unexpected. We didn't realise we would click the way we did and form the fan base we did as a duo. We just had a great chemistry with music and people could always tell. We vibed off each other really well. We were fans of one another and we just loved doing those covers together. It was only after we linked up together that we started seeing growth and success. Before we partnered up, we both had less than 100 subscribers on YouTube, as well as receiving less than a 100 views on each of our videos. After we covered "OMG" and saw our success as a duo, we continued and everything blew up after that.'

Conor added: 'He's now a really close friend, but back then I didn't know him. He sent me a message saying he would like to work with me. I checked him out, and wow, this guy was crazy! He was really talented and I thought okay, let's do a song together. At that time, everyone was asking me to cover Usher's "OMG". I had never really covered that many current songs. I was doing Stevie Wonder, all those songs I listened to growing up. I said to him, "All my friends are asking me to cover Usher's 'OMG'. I've done Usher's part but I've got no one to do Will.i.am's part. I don't know any other singers, would you rap instead?" And he sent me a message saying, "Yo, We should do a video for it. I've noticed you haven't done any videos. I think we should do a video to make it more interesting."

'I was a little bit nervous because I had never done that before. I was like, let's do it.'

Finding his mother's digital camera and standing it on top of a pile of books, a young Conor took his first step into unknown territory. Anth explained about this process: 'Our first video together was a cover of Usher and Will.i.am's "OMG". Conor recorded his vocals first, and then sent me his vocals, as well as the empty verse for me to record mine over. I finished recording my vocals, and sent them all back to Conor to edit all the audio together into one track. Once we finished the vocals, Conor uploaded the video of the audio with just a picture on it to his channel.

'Later that week, I thought it would be cool to record a video for it, I noticed Conor had never recorded a video for YouTube before, so I figured this could be a cool first time to do it. I messaged Conor via YouTube asking him if he was up for the idea, and he loved it. I then filmed myself lip-syncing my rap for the cover and then Conor sent me his video of him lip-syncing his parts. Took us both plenty of takes since it was pretty new to us. Then it was my job to edit our videos together into one and have it ready to upload for YouTube. Funnily enough, we followed the exact same process for every YouTube video we did together after that one.'

The video for 'OMG' may have been his first one, but it was clear Conor was a natural. His trademark finger-pointing during the beats is evident, as is the casual smirk and natural energy. There doesn't seem to be any nerves as he leans in closely to the microphone, crooning against the white backdrop of his bedroom wall.

'I found my mother's digital camera and set it up. I actually made a video camera stand by piling the camera on books and stood in front of the microphone. I put it up online and forgot about it,' said Conor.

As the tracks grew more and more popular, he became something of a celebrity at school, with many of his fellow pupils in awe of the aspiring pop star in their midst. But there were also negative undertones, with Conor admitting in one interview that not everyone liked what he was doing – 'Most people were supportive, and those that weren't, who's laughing now?'

The few hundred views that he received soon became millions, thanks to his covers of more modern popular tracks such as 'OMG' and Ne-Yo's 'Beautiful Monster'. Anth said: 'To be honest, we NEVER thought that would happen! I remember us not really paying attention to the video after it being uploaded because we never received any views or comments on any of our previous videos, so we thought this one would be no different, but we were definitely wrong, haha. The next time we looked at the video, it had over 100,000 views and hundreds and hundreds of comments. Both of our YouTube channels had shot up to over 1,000 subscribers and they were increasing daily by the hundreds. It all happened so fast; it was crazy.'

He continued to this author: 'The huge reaction was just so unexpected. We didn't really know what to do, haha. We just couldn't believe the amount of views we were getting. We always thought it'd be impossible to get views like that and here we were, two teenagers doing covers out of their bedroom, getting millions of views on YouTube, haha. It was just so unreal. I remember us both still being in school and talking on Skype about how we even started getting Facebook requests from random strangers because they were "fans". It was all so new to us, actually having fans, haha. We both even reached the 5,000-person friend limit on Facebook – that was hilarious to us. We were getting tons of blogs and articles written about us and our YouTube covers from different websites all over the world. Even getting recognition from the artists themselves of whose songs we were covering, such as Chris Brown tweeting our cover of "Yeah 3x" and giving us props for it. And before we knew it, we started getting emails and messages from managers and record label executives.'

Conor added in another interview: 'I was telling my mum and dad I was getting lots of hits on the internet and they were like, "Great, do your geography homework". It was hard to explain to people. People started to realise, and my Facebook page became a fan page. It kept growing and growing.

'I didn't realise what it really meant. I hit two million, five million, 10 million. At school, people would joke that "It's almost like you're famous."

'When we first came on the scene everyone looked at us as a duo act because no one had ever seen us before, and we came out together. We were like, we should just go with this – people are liking this. They love the music. I was like, we might as well keep doing the covers.'

Anth added: 'We both always worked together equally, we both always gave the same amount of input. It was always just funny to us how we would always have the same ideas for songs and how we would do the video. If Conor would ever suggest a song to cover, I would trust him as he would with me. It was always a song that we both liked, or a song that we thought we could really make different and make our own. Especially covering a song like "Motherlover" by The Lonely Island. I still remember how hesitant Conor was to do that cover when I first had the idea. It was about 4am US time and 9am UK time; I called him and woke him up to get on Skype because I had an idea on what we can cover next. I told him the song so he could listen to it. He loved it and thought it was hilarious but he thought I was crazy, haha. It was just so weird how we clicked when it came to music, always having the same ideas and taste in music.'

Anth continued: 'Conor's my best friend, my brother, my family. We've been through EVERYTHING together. Whether it be from career problems to girl problems. We've always had each other's back with everything, since the very beginning. It's just crazy how many things we have in common. We always have a great time when we hang out – we'll make a good time out of any situation or work. The amount of inside jokes we have are endless, and they're all probably really dumb, but we think they're the funniest things ever, haha. He's also the ONLY guy I know, besides me, who could eat Chipotle or Nando's every single day and never get sick or tired of it, haha. I remember people would always think we'd drift apart as time went on, but it never happened. If anything, this entire journey has only gotten us closer. Even now, we still talk every single day. I'll always get a phone call from him on the daily or vice versa. Even if it's just to say what's up or how the day is going, we always keep in touch no matter what.'

Uploading content included 'Crawl' by Chris Brown, Taio Cruz's 'Dynamite' and 'Only Girl (In The World)' by Rihanna.

Conor told *4Music.com* about his choice of covers: 'I was definitely a fan of Bruno Mars when I started doing his covers. But I was also a fan of Chris Brown, Usher, Justin Timberlake, Ne-Yo. I covered a massive variety of different songs, so I never had a specific artist that I considered my favourite. I just covered songs regardless of who they were. If it was a good song I'd cover it, and that is how I went about choosing which covers I did.'

While his covers were seen by music fans and quickly attracted a loyal fan base, his work was also being noticed in the industry. But at the moment he was just trying to secure his relationship with the fans. On replying to comments, he said: 'I try to, I used to try to reply to each one, which now would take the rest of my life so I don't do it anymore. I love reading ones where they say how much they love the cover, that they enjoyed it. As long as they're enjoying it, it's cool. I always try and keep up with what fans are thinking and what they want next. YouTube is ruthless. The ones where it is constructive criticism, you take that on board and you think, right, next cover I'm going to show them what they want me to do. But sometimes it's just stupid, but I think I'm very lucky, because the amazing comments outweigh those kinds of comments.'

His mum was less than happy with one particular comment, though. Conor said: 'I remember really early on, I was only doing covers and I was sent a message from a woman who claimed that her first child was conceived whilst listening to one of my songs, so that was a nice little story that I read out to my mum on Facebook, not realising what it said whilst I was reading it. I was like, "Oh look, I've got fan mail, Mum" and she said, "Don't read fan mail to me ever again, Conor." I do get given lots of crazy things.'

He added: 'I grew up listening to Michael Jackson, Stevie Wonder, Usher, Ne-Yo, Justin Timberlake... their vocals inspire me. If people want to say that there's something they don't like about me, I think that's fine. As long as they can't say that I can't sing, that's all that matters to me. I wouldn't really care if someone said, "Oh, I don't like the way he looks." For me, it's all about the music.'

During those covers there was one in particular that was an explosive success: 'I remember we hit our first million views with Ne-Yo "Beautiful Monster", which was mad – we kept ramping up the views. At that moment it was just a very online thing; I was famous online.

'It was a weird situation for them [his friends], because they didn't really get it – "You get lots of views, do you make any money from them?"

'I think the moment [when things changed] was when I was getting sent contracts. It was really weird to get messages on YouTube saying: "I've seen your stuff, I'm a manager from America, I'd love to sign you" – all these kinds of things. I'd be like, what does this mean? I started getting contracts from people all over the world. I showed it to my mum, saying can you read this? So we sought help from a music lawyer.'

The lawyer studied Conor's collection of music videos on YouTube and rang back, saying: 'I think he can do better than that.'

During his covers, Conor decided to leave college to pursue his musical career. He recalled: 'I had just started my second year at college [doing Geography, ICT, Media Studies and Music Technology] and I didn't know what to do. So I spoke to my mum and I spoke to the college, and we all thought the best choice was just to go for it.

'I do remember when I did leave college, I was scared that I was going to get kicked out because if this didn't go well, I would wanna go back and I thought maybe I should just tell them what's going on. So I told the head of my college and he was like, look, you need to chase it if this is what you want to do, but if things go wrong you're welcome to come back and I said okay. But obviously I didn't go back because everything has worked out for me. For me I think it would be quite hard to do education at the same time since there's like a million people that wanna do the same thing as me right now and wanna be in the position I'm in, so I've gotta keep my eye on the ball before someone takes it. I've gotta put, like,

110 per cent of my focus into what I'm doing. I did my AS-levels so I did get quite far before I went into music.'

He added in another interview: 'I was in the middle of college, doing A-levels when it really kicked off. I would probably be at university if I wasn't doing this; it would have been really fun to go to uni – I look at my friends at uni and think it would have been really fun to go to uni, but they are looking back at me and thinking the same thing!'

His original plan was to 'finish college, then have a gap year to try and do something with my music, but it all happened early. Maybe I'd have studied geography at uni – I quite liked it at school.'

He was contacted via Facebook by someone claiming to be on Ne-Yo's management team. Conor told the *Telegraph*: 'I wanted to believe it, but my parents were in my ears, "You don't know who he is, he could be anyone." So I plucked up the courage to say, "I don't mean to be rude but is there any proof that you even know Ne-Yo?"'

He told *Teen Vogue*: 'I started to receive random messages over the internet from managers and record labels trying to get in touch with me. I didn't really believe any of it, so I just ignored a lot of them. Suddenly, out of nowhere, I got this message on Facebook from somebody saying that they knew Ne-Yo and that he checked out one of my covers and really liked it. The person said Ne-Yo wanted to fly me out to America. I thought, I don't even know if he knows Ne-Yo. Is there any proof at all? Is this one of my friends pulling a prank? A few days after I asked for proof, and I was suddenly on Skype with Ne-Yo, talking to him about music. He told me that he wanted to sign me, and then I got to meet with a few different record labels. Eventually, I signed my first record label in the UK.'

Conor told BBC Radio 1's Nick Grimshaw: 'I was in London and I got this text, "Do you have Skype? Ne-Yo wants to Skype you". I was like, this is the worst timing, can you wait a few hours? They were like, "Uh, okay. He's meant to be out but we will try to make him wait." I got home at 10pm. I wrote, "I'm really sorry for the wait. Is there any way he can still do it?" They replied: "He's gone out, but he's coming back." What if it's not him? Should I wear pyjamas to make it look casual? So, if it's not him I could say I didn't believe him anyway.'

Conor waited until 1am for his phone call from the pop superstar, sitting in his bedroom in his pyjamas, anxiously hoping that it would all be true. When the call finally came, he still had to keep quiet during the surreal chat in case he woke his parents!

'It was about midnight when I was on Skype to him, everyone in my house was asleep,' he told the *Associated Press*. 'So I was like, "Hi, Ne-Yo." That kind of killed any starstruckness – I had to talk really quietly.'

He added to Radio 1's Nick Grimshaw: 'It was hilarious because it was such a random experience. I got a call one day from his manager again, saying, "Yo, Ne-Yo is in London. He wants to meet you. He's at the Mayfair Hotel." I was given a number to ring when I get there. I'm in the lobby and I'm just waiting there. And I ring this number I've been given – I think it's his tour manager. And I was told, "What you wearing?" And I was like, "What, I'm not here for this kind of thing." Then I realised they need to find me. I think the second time I met him was the more serious one; it was the day after. I'm on the way home and I get the call – he really likes you. He thinks you are cool. He wants to meet you again, 10am.

'This time there is a big camera there, his security guard is standing outside. He walks me in, and he was like, "I'm really serious about signing you. I want to sign you." He was like, "I want to hear you sing live." I didn't know what to sing, I didn't know any warm-up techniques – I didn't know what to do. I've just got to wing it, and I think I sung "Nothing On You" by Bruno Mars.

'He had a smile on his face and I thought, "Phew I did it!" Then he just kind of said, "Yeah, let's do it." Obviously, that's what sparked the crazy UK labels.'

Conor decided not to sign with Ne-Yo, however. He explained his reasons to *Flavoursome*: 'I thought about it, I wasn't just like, "Oh my God, it's Ne-Yo, nobody tell me not to sign with him!" I mean, I listened to people around me who knew about contracts better than I did, people who were looking out for my best interests. Whereas that just wasn't in my best interests, I would have had to move to America. I was only 17, I would have had to leave my family because they couldn't have come with me; I have a younger brother and sister. It would have been a massive jump when I had other offers that were better and easier. And it was never done in a bad way; I explained to them how I felt and Ne-Yo's now featuring on the album and has written an incredible song for it. There were never any grudges; it was very clear why it needed to be done.'

Ne-Yo, whose real name is Shaffer Chimere

Smith, first began his music career as a songwriter before finally stepping out in front of the microphone. The Grammy award-winning singer released his debut album, *In My Own Words*, in 2006 and has gone on to enjoy huge success. But Ne-Yo wasn't the only music superstar interested in signing Conor Maynard.

Pharrell Williams is a charismatic singer, who became famous for his songwriting work during his time as one half of the producing and songwriting duo Neptunes. Among the tracks they worked on are Britney Spears' 'I'm A Slave 4 U' and 'There She Goes' by Babyface. In 2003, Williams released his first solo single, 'Frontin''. He also found fame with his rock and funk hybrid group N.E.R.D.

Said Conor: 'Both Pharrell and Ne-Yo found me on the Web and followed my stuff. Ne-Yo reached out, and we talked on Skype and then Ne-Yo told me he wanted to sign me, which started a buzz around the UK, like, "Who is this young kid that Ne-Yo wants to sign?" and then later down the line Pharrell got in contact (after I was signed) saying he'd love to work with me, and so I went to Miami for a week to work in his studio.

'I saw more famous people then than I have in my whole life. Ludacris was in the studio. Tyler, the Creator, Lil Wayne – it was an incredible time and I can't believe I got to work with Pharrell. He said he thinks I'm going to change the future of pop music. That was a big line from the Pharrell-meister!'

He added to *AOL.com*: 'I did get quite a little quote from Pharrell Williams. I was in the studio with him in Miami. It was the most amazing experience and yeah, he sat me down and said that's how he felt. It was really, really cool.'

Conor told Scottish newspaper the *Daily Record* about his relationship with Ne-Yo: 'He is a cool guy. He's very kind and treats me like an equal artist, even though it's early in my career.'

Ne-Yo said of Conor to the *Daily Star*: 'I don't feel like he's a copycat of Justin Bieber. That's what being a human being is all about – we categorize things. But Conor is going to be around long enough for people to go, "That's Conor Maynard", as opposed to, "He sounds like Bieber".

'He's a young white kid with a soulful voice so of course that comparison is expected, but he will stand the test of time. Conor is amazing. He has the talent, the potential of those guys like Marvin [Gaye] and The Temptations. His tone is insane. It's really, really rare that I come across a person that has a tone I wish I had, and he's a good kid mentally. That's too few and far between.

'Everyone has an ego these days but you have to do something to validate that ego. But not him – he's having fun, he's not taking the world too serious. I dig that. I told him to cling onto that.'

Ne-Yo also insisted he believes Conor will be around for a long time as he doesn't take fame too seriously.

Conor is still in touch with Ne-Yo – telling *TheArtsDesk*: 'Over in New York last week, still definitely working on music. I see him whenever I'm in New York or he's in London – a really cool guy, almost a mentor in terms of my music. We just chill in the studio, really – talking and eating. I also went along to his little Malibu Red party to hang out so that was cool.'

In 2013, following his amazing success in 2012, Ne-Yo told Yahoo that he was delighted with the progress of his young protégé. However, he knows of the pitfalls that come with reaching so much success at a young age. Expressing concern, he added: 'I'm extremely proud of that dude, I'm now concerned about the parts of the business that have the tendency to distract.

'You've got young ladies screaming your name now which beforehand maybe wasn't the case.

You've got people in your face now. I've always appreciated and respected Conor's level-headedness. I pray that he keeps it. I make sure that I do my part and give him a call every now and then and say, "Hey, keep it about the music, take care of that throat, don't do anything stupid and you'll be around for a while because people are digging what you do – don't screw it up."'

When told that Ne-Yo was worried that Conor could get distracted by the opposite sex, Conor said to *Yahoo! OMG!*: 'Well too late – I've been distracted – no I'm joking. No I'll definitely be cool, it's hard you know, there are a lot of lovely ladies around. It's fun, for me I try to make the most out of every situation and have as much fun as I can. I've been meeting so many people on my travels.'

And he met up with his old mentor once more after he was added to the bill for Ne-Yo's U.K. tour in March 2013. It began in Newcastle's Metro Radio Arena on 6 March, and Conor found himself joining up with *X Factor* star Tulisa Contostavlos.

The tour was to promote Ne-Yo's latest album *R.E.D.* Ne-Yo said about the album: 'It came from me stepping outside myself, looking at my life as it is today and realising that every dream I've had from the day I decided I wanted to do music, every dream that I've had from then till now, I'm definitely on the way to realising it.'

As Conor's popularity continued to grow, so did a tag that would soon follow him wherever he went. With his cute puppy dog looks and winsome charm, coupled with unwavering ambition and a canny insight into how to be noticed, it was no shock that he would be compared to Justin Bieber. In fact, no interview with Conor is complete without a question about Bieber.

Both of these musical talents were first seen on YouTube, bringing them out into the open and creating easy access to their fans via Twitter – a far cry from the usual restrictions pop stars have with their record-buying public. Instead they could have instant rapport with those who like their music and build up an immediate relationship.

With Conor constantly compared to Justin Bieber, especially before his debut album was released, it's important to take a look at his rival star's world.

Justin Drew Bieber was born on 1 March 1994 in Stratford, Ontario, Canada. A self-confessed regular kid, who likes to hang out with his friends and play sport, Bieber's world, much like Conor's, was dominated by music. His dad played the guitar, while his mother sung – and it rubbed off on the young Canadian. By the age of 12 he could play piano, guitar, drums and trumpet. And he could sing as well.

After coming second in a local singing talent competition when he was 12, Bieber's mum decided to post videos of his performance on YouTube so family and friends who were unable to attend wouldn't miss out. Bieber, who spent his free time busking around Stratford, would have had no idea just what was going to happen following the videos being uploaded.

After hundreds of thousands of views, more videos of Justin were uploaded and it was not too long before he was fast becoming a social media phenomenon. A hip-hop producer named Scooter Braun was surfing the Net, wading through countless videos of amateur singers, hoping to find the next musical talent. As soon as he saw Bieber's videos in 2008 he knew that he had finally found what he was looking for. After calling three school boards in Justin's area, he located the boy. The school board immediately got in touch with Justin's mother, Pattie, who, despite being initially reluctant, warmed to Scooter after a long chat.

He signed Justin shortly after and soon attracted two of the biggest music stars. Justin Timberlake wanted to sign him to his own label, Tennman

Records, after the former N-Sync star heard Bieber sing a cover of his own hit, 'Cry Me A River', saying: 'I think he's a great guy and I hope to collaborate with him in the future.' However, it was Usher who won the bidding war, and in 2009 Bieber's debut EP, *My World*, was released, breaking Billboard records.

Usher told *The L.A. Times*: 'I think it was, first and foremost, his charming, winning, timeless attitude. It's as though he had been here before. When I met him, his personality won me over. When he sang, I realized we were dealing with the real thing. His voice just spoke to the type of music I would want to be associated with. And it wasn't a gimmick – we had to teach him how to dance and be on stage, but he really had a good voice.'

Recalling how he met Bieber, Usher added: 'He was there in the parking lot of Jermaine Dupri's studio, so of course I knew that Scooter [Braun], his manager, was there meeting Jermaine. And Justin offered to sing for me. But I didn't want to intrude on anything going on, and I thought it would be disrespectful to have him sing for me there. I wanted to arrange a meeting at another place and time so we'd have an opportunity for us to really talk and not just rush through it. I told him to come inside, because it was very cold outside and he wanted to sing for me right then, right there! Which is so funny because I can remember being that same kid. I'd speak to Keith Sweat and other artists when I was a kid.'

He added: 'I reached back out to Scooter, and we arranged a meeting. After watching his videos online, I thought, man, this kid has an incredible voice! I'd like to see him in person. To my surprise, he was everything I thought he would be. Being able to play guitar and all of those things were a great foundation for him. I thought, given his confident understanding, that we could teach him how to play to a large audience and get ready for videos, and that this could be a success.

'It was Justin Timberlake first. I'd almost missed the boat, and Justin was scheduled to meet Justin Timberlake in L.A. with Jimmy Iovine. So I said, "I really believe in this kid's talent, and I have what it takes to introduce him in the right way. I want to give a wealth of information to him. I understand the process you're gonna go through, and going through vocal changes. I understand what it is to go from scratch and his passion, and how to nurture who he is." And, luckily, he trusted me – was enough of a fan of mine – to take a shot.'

In a 2011 interview, Scooter said of Bieber's rise to fame: 'I don't think it was a short period of time

– we built his YouTube channel over three years. He had a bigger YouTube channel before we even did a record deal with Usher. All the statistics pointed at the internet, and kids are spending more time on the internet as opposed to TV and radio; the mainstream didn't realize the impact because there wasn't validity till Justin became big. YouTube is bare bones and all we did was use a flip video camera.'

And Scooter didn't hold back on the praise: 'Justin is truly talented; he is that special superstar that you see once in a lifetime. He plays four instruments, self-taught. He showed that in his YouTube channel. He had an incredible tone in his voice. He was captivating and I think that the marketing was right. At the end of the day, the secret to the marketing was to keep it organic and authentic. Make the kids realize that it's theirs. Don't overproduce the videos. Don't try and put in special editing. Just let the kid sing and play his guitar and if he's the real deal the kids will run with it because they'll feel like it's theirs, and have their own self-discovery.'

Despite his belief in the young singer, Scooter revealed there were obstacles in his way, admitting: 'The obstacles were that people didn't want to sign him because he didn't have a Disney or

Nickelodeon show, and because no one had ever broken in through YouTube. Justin Timberlake had the biggest YouTube star in the world, Esmee Denters, and it hadn't worked yet. Ryan Leslie had that other girl and that didn't work. There was no validity and no proven track record. The only ways minors have broken over the past years was through having their own Disney or Nickelodeon show, and every label told me that unless I had a TV show attached to one of those networks, they were not interested whatsoever.'

However, he warned that just being a hit on YouTube doesn't necessarily guarantee chart success: 'We were very strategic with how we introduced stuff and when we introduced it. I think we also fed the hunger. I think we had our finger on the pulse because we communicated directly with the consumer, with the fans. We let them tell us what they wanted at the time and constantly kept surprising them, and we kept our word, and that's the most important thing. As Justin has become bigger and bigger, we haven't left them behind: he continues to tweet often, post YouTube videos, and spends time on Facebook.

'I'll give you an example. We were in Australia for the first time ever, and everything was shut down. Here we are in Australia and everybody wants to meet Justin – every press outlet, everyone. And we get a Twitter sent to me and Justin by @JBSource. The two girls who created it were coming. We know @JBSource because they have over 90,000 followers – they are one of Justin's biggest fan clubs. The girl seeks me out. She goes, "I'm JBSource, is it possible to interview Justin for our Twitter page, and a video interview we can post for the kids?" I went to the label and they said absolutely not. They said, "Absolutely not, we've already turned down over 100 different outlets; we have no time for these kids." I said, "I don't think you guys get it. Unless they get an interview, we aren't doing anything because they are the most important interview we're going to do here." We cancelled some big outlet and we brought in the kid, with her dad and her two friends. They videotaped an interview with Justin, that he loved doing because he knew who they were. And that's his favourite thing – communicating directly to the fans. That video was one of the biggest-seen videos of that week; that was the video that all the fans watched. They aren't going on to read some dot com news site. They wanted to go see what the other girl said: she met Justin, what he said to her.'

He added: 'The secret is keeping it organic. When I see people say that Justin is part of this machine: no, he isn't. If my one laptop and my camera is a machine, then yes, it is. There was no other marketing behind it. It was my laptop, a flip camera, and Justin and his laptop. We don't give them passwords to anything. Justin does it himself and we create our own content.

'We keep it organic, and that's our secret. The only other secret is that he has something special that cannot be taught – that's the real superstar stuff. And you see it, not only with him generating traffic, but you can see it when he takes the stage and I'm nervous that he can't sing because he's tired. When he broke his leg, he said, "Don't worry, I'm performing tomorrow. Tell Taylor I'm not cancelling." He went out there with a broken foot and a cast and performed an entire show at Manchester Stadium, and then over the next three weeks did 14 radio shows with a broken foot. People still talk about him rocking Madison Square Garden last year, and they forgot that he had a broken foot. He didn't cancel one show and he's 16 years old. That's real superstar stuff!'

Another fan is music mogul Simon Cowell, who stated: 'The genius of Justin Bieber is he used the power of social media like no other artist – and he doesn't stop. Only a fool would underestimate him. I've met him a few times: he's bright. The kid is more in charge than people think. I know this industry, I know what it takes, and he will be around for a very long time.'

Justin Bieber is certainly keeping his eye on the prize, and his work ethic and determination to stay on top mirrors similar traits to Conor.

Bieber said in 2012: 'I never stop working. In what I wanted to do in music, I've never had any fear but now I'm at the top there's nowhere to go but down. For me it's about staying standing at the top.

'I'm not a kid any more – I'm an adult, I'm making the decisions and I want to keep on growing, and I believe I can. I look at Justin Timberlake and Usher and see how they crossed over really successfully, and I've seen people go off at the deep end, get full of themselves, think they're the best and end up not being anything. I've worked way too hard for that.

'I definitely don't want to be just another teen heart-throb but there are different ways of growing. I want to be loved like Michael Jackson was, from the four-year-olds to the 80-year-olds.

'I am going to change and grow through my music and doing films.'

In another comparison of Conor to Bieber, Ne-

Yo also had a chance to sign the youngster. He said in 2010: 'Justin did a cover of one of my songs on YouTube, which created a buzz. He came to a show and performed, and was incredible then but I didn't do anything because he was 11.'

And he added: 'I have no regrets. Things happen for a reason – he wasn't supposed to be signed to me. Usher has done good: where he is now is where he's meant to be. I still feel like he's figuring out things. Once he gets some tangible records, he'll be a force to be reckoned with. Ten years from now, no one will be singing "Baby". It's good, but not very memorable. Justin is great on the drums and the guitar. He has talent and potential to land up there with Justin Timberlake and co. Talent will take you further than looks, than how flat your stomach is.'

The comparisons to Justin Bieber have long been mooted and it should come as no surprise that record labels were looking for a British version. Conor himself said of the comparisons: 'I can see why – we're both young and came through YouTube. But I don't like being boxed in. I would much rather people listened to the album and made up their own mind rather than being told what it is. I think my music is aimed at a slightly older and more sophisticated palette. I named the album *Contrast* because I wanted to show it wasn't a Bieber 2.0 album.

'A lot of people had it in their minds that I was the next Justin Bieber but I didn't want to follow anyone. I had to find out what kind of an artist I was because I had never been in a studio, I hadn't even written a song. I had this motto, "It's better to fail in originality than to succeed in imitation".'

He added: 'I wanted to put my own unique stamp on everything because that was how I was successful on YouTube. I took covers and switched them up and did it my own way, and people became a fan of me rather than a fan of the songs. That was crazy, I didn't realise what it really meant. I hit two million, five million, 10 million – I was happy with a few hundred views a month. Just like that.'

Conor has also been compared to Justin Timberlake. However, he remarked: 'Comparisons in general, you know, I'm not really trying to be the next Justin Timberlake. I'm not really trying to be the next anything. For me it's all about being the first Conor Maynard. Timberlake was a massive influence for me growing up, but at the same time I still think it's a different thing. I think there are some songs on the album that you wouldn't really hear him doing. Some songs would fit [with making that comparison], but some really don't. Even when I was creating my album, I suppose, the motto I went with was that it's better to fail in originality than it is to succeed in imitation. I wasn't trying to copy anyone else – I was trying to be as original as possible.'

He is a fan of Timberlake, though, and couldn't resist commenting on his return to music. The first single from the album *The 20/20 Experience* is his first album in seven years and the lead single, 'Suit and Tie', was released in early 2013.

Conor said of the song: 'It was really weird, though – I heard the first 20 seconds and I was a bit like, "What has he done?!" Like, did he hear it before he put it out? But then I realised the rest of it is just crazy. I was in America when I first heard it, and all the American radio stations just cut off that first bit and just played the rest of the song. It's kind of cheating, though really, isn't it? 'Cos it's not the real song.'

Despite the comparisons, Conor was clearly his own person. This was doubly impressive, especially as he had released only cover versions. However, he was praised for making each cover his own and not just copying previous work. Of making the best cover version, he said: 'You need to really switch it up and make it your own. Show off your own style and uniqueness to stand out. That's the advice I'd give to people getting started online now.'

Not all his covers were well received by everyone, though. One of his ex-girlfriends said that his version of Snow Patrol's 'Chasing Cars' is the only cover that she liked. They broke up after he moved from Brighton, but he admits that he was hurt by the comments.

He said: 'That ended because I moved away from Brighton to London, but I do remember her saying that and me thinking, "Thanks, I work really hard on these covers, actually."'

Conor was still doing his best to ensure that he was at the forefront of cutting-edge technology in 2011 – teaming up with BT Infinity for the first of a series of live streamed performances on YouTube at the Live From the 34th Floor.

He said: 'I'm doing a live stream with BT Infinity and I think it's a really, really cool idea. I mean, it's obvious with me because it really relates to how I started. My whole project started online, I built my fan base online and this whole thing that I'm doing today is all about BT Infinity, this crazy fast broadband that makes it easier for all my fans to be online and allows them to watch me perform live over the internet.

'So it's a really cool thing that I'm able to do. I

always like to do performances or shows for my fans that really relate to how I started, and almost inspire them to go away and learn from it and do what they want. 'It's really cool. It's back to the beginning, back to my roots and I think it's a really nice way to come back and almost literally showing them how it happened for me.'

He said of YouTube: 'Well, I went through the whole YouTube route and I'd say that is a very good platform for people to use. I think if you're gonna go through that route it's a lot more difficult now because everyone knows about it and everyone does it. But for me, with covering songs, if you're gonna do it you need to really take it and make it your own, even if you need to change the melody, change the lyrics or style of the song. Just do what you need to do to make it you!'

Conor told *FlavourMag.co.uk*: 'Use YouTube as a platform. But a lot of people know that, and a lot of people do that. What worked when I did it was, you've got to take a song but no matter what you do, you've got to make it your own – in your own way, your own style, whether you change the lyrics or the melody, whatever it takes to make people become a fan of you rather than the song. That's when people start to respect you as an artist.'

He tweeted: 'A lot of people always message me

saying they want to be a singer, but it's too hard so they might just give up, so imam [sic] say this, Standing at the bottom of a mountain, you have to go through the struggle of the climb to know what it feels like to touch the sky.'

Conor continues to release covers. In January 2013, he gave fans a Happy New Year Treat by releasing his latest cover of Swedish House Mafia's 'Don't You Worry Child'.

He has become such a star that people now cover his own songs. Giving his social networking cover roots, it's a new thing for Conor. 'It's a weird feeling,' he admits. 'But there was this girl that did a cover of "Can't Say No" that was so cool – she switched it up. That's what I did with my covers – I switched it up and made it different. So, whenever other people do that, it's really cool.'

Conor continues to make sure that his success doesn't harm interaction with his fans (sometimes when a star becomes famous, they can close themselves off from their fans). However, he continues to tweet regularly, keeping his fans aware of everything that has happened to him during his amazing journey to pop stardom. Ever the canny promoter, he's also aware that his fans can also double up as his social networking promoters. He regularly asks them to trend his latest single or a piece of news. There is also a regular video diary update that he uploads to YouTube, entitled *The Conorcles*.

He told *Flavour Mag*: 'That was kind of a joint idea between myself and a load of people. We were trying to work out the difficult step to go from recording videos in my bedroom to having a real music video and like, "Oh, I'm a real artist now," it's difficult to show that transition. So I thought *The Conorcles* were a good way of showing the fans exactly what I was doing and how I was making that transition, that I'm with them every step of the way.'

And Anth Melo still hopes for more collaboration: 'Most definitely! We always talk about continuing our YouTube collaborations together, as well as releasing more originals and more features on his upcoming albums. We always end up working on music one way or another when we're together.'

CHAPTER THREE

CAPITALISING ON THE HYPE

Conor Maynard wasn't the first person to grab people's attention with their music ability through the internet. Over the last few years, it has become a hugely popular tool, allowing wannabe chart superstars to showcase their talents without the aid of big music industry labels.

One of the first big successes, certainly in Britain anyway, was Lily Allen. Lily was a singer signed up to a record label but struggling to find her sound. After being told that she needed to work with other producers, she decided to upload the songs that she had already completed on to MySpace.

They first appeared in November 2005, and she seemed to enjoy the feedback. Within three months, it was clear that her records were finding an audience, and it was getting to the point that she would finish working on a song and then put it up on MySpace five minutes later.

She said to *Pitchfork* in 2006: 'It was obvious that something was going on because there were so many subscribers to the blog and so many people listening to the music – the plays were just going up and up and up.

'I signed to Regal, a division of Polygram for £25,000. It was like nothing – a really, really small development deal. At that time they were putting out a Kylie album, a Coldplay album, the Gorillaz album had just been released. So, they didn't really care about me. They were happy with me – they signed me – but at that point my album wasn't meant to come out in England until this coming January [2007]. So, they didn't really have a plan, so to speak. They didn't think that the direction of the demos was quite right. It wasn't that they weren't supportive; they just didn't think it was ready because it wasn't.'

She added: 'They were trying things out, like putting me with more mainstream producers and top-line writers because they didn't think my melodies were quite there – it wasn't sonically "pop sounding" enough or whatever. You know within a record company they have A&R and marketing and press and whatever. Obviously, A&R knew about me but nobody else in the record company did at that point. And Murray [Chalmers], the head of press, was getting calls from people who were like, "We want to write about Lily," and he was like, "I don't know what you're talking about."

'The *Observer Music Monthly* magazine were like, "We're writing an article about MySpace and we want to do a thing on Lily." Murray was like, "OK, this is stupid. Now five people have called about this Lily girl, who the hell is she?" So he walked down to A&R and was like, "Have we got someone called Lily Allen on our books?" And they were like, "Oh yeah, she's this girl we got a few months ago." And that's kind of when it all started, and then three weeks later we got the offer for the [*OMM*] cover.'

Lily's huge success, thanks to MySpace, caused a big stir and the press were naturally eager to find the new star on the internet. Other acts followed, and it seemed MySpace and Bebo were going to be most popular sites for new music acts to show off their talent.

Bebo's Sarah Gavin said in 2006: 'It's really powerful. I think it's the first time that individuals have got the power.

'We've got authors up there publicising their books. If they're just starting out as a film producer they have the opportunity to get their content up on the site and go out to the general public to see what they actually think about it. It's a hugely powerful medium and people are just starting to grasp how effective that can be.'

However, MySpace's fall was almost as quick as its rise. Its success attracted the scourge of popular internet sites – spammers – and those who had been using it for years, witnessed it becoming corporate. MySpace was sold to Rupert Murdoch for nearly $600 million in 2005.

However, a brand new website would soon jump from being just a site on which you could watch crazy home videos, to something more. Anth said of YouTube: 'I think the internet is very important for aspiring artists, especially YouTube. It's a new way to get your name out there without any help from a label or management. You can build your own fan base and career straight from your bedroom. I think it's the greatest platform you can have today to get your name out to people all around the world. I think people underestimate how powerful the internet really is. We [himself and Conor] would both not be where we were today if it wasn't for the internet and YouTube. I think people should see the success that Conor has had from the internet and YouTube and learn from it and be inspired by it. It really does show you that anything is possible. You can literally go from making videos in your bedroom to becoming an international pop star and having your very own book written about you, haha.'

In any case, YouTube sensations were nothing new. Justin Bieber is the major success, but there have been several others – some not finding chart success as easy as success with fans on the internet. One of the best recent YouTube successes is Karmin – an acoustic and hip-hop blend that has become a social networking phenomenon, comprising Amy Heidemann and Nick Noonan.

Amy told *The L.A Times*: 'We performed in a couple of different groups and realised how difficult it was for everyone to be on the same page. You see bands like U2 that have been together forever, and it's so rare to find that. So, we were like, "Hey, we make great songs together." We'd heard that it was a bad idea as a couple to work together, so we were worried about that, but we just decided to jump into it.'

Talking about YouTube, Amy said: 'The music industry is so different than how it used to be – it's not just about records anymore. There's so many other facets that we can dive into, and you never really run out of things to pursue. On YouTube, for example, I've got hair tutorials totally unrelated to music, but it's just part of what we do. It's just part of who I am. Nick will probably have a sports blog later. But, it was our manager, Nils Gums, that got us onto YouTube. He knows it very well, and it's actually the number two search engine in the world behind Google. He said that we should start doing cover songs on YouTube because that will grab people's attention. For example, if you cover Chris Brown and people are searching for him, yours pops up in the search, so they kind of stumble upon you. You grab people's attention that aren't really searching for you.'

As for talking about the future of YouTube, Nick added: 'We plan on continuing to do covers. We like doing covers because it's fun and pushes us creatively, believe it or not, to do a completely different version of a song. And it's good practice. So, we're gonna continue to do that for a little while just because it's also cool for the fans.'

Conor and Karmin inadvertently crossed paths, with Conor looking out of his hotel room during his 'Vegas Girl' shoot to see them playing an outside gig in early 2012.

The YouTube successes didn't surprise Scooter Braun – manager of Justin Bieber. He told *Forbes.com*: 'I signed Justin and Asher Roth when they weren't popular online. I signed Justin when he had 70,000 views on YouTube, not 50 million. I signed Asher Roth when he had 60 friends on his MySpace. So the answer is absolutely because I did it with these two. My philosophy was that you could build them online. I'm not someone who jumped in and said, "Look at what they have, let me chase them!" This is something that we built from the ground up together. Asher Roth lived on my couch for six months to build up a following. With Justin Bieber, I moved him and his mother to a town house a block away from me.

'I'm filming half of those videos you see online. The answer is absolutely yes. I signed these guys with the same feeling in my gut they were stars, just like anyone would sign acts before. My philosophy on how I break them and how I exposed them to the world was just different than anyone else's. Everyone told me I was nuts. Everyone said no to both my acts. Everyone said no, you're nuts and you can't do it this way. These acts aren't going to work. No one has broken two acts from scratch in over a decade other than *American Idol*. What we introduced was a new philosophy showing that if the number one retailer in music is iTunes, then why shouldn't the number one marketing avenue be the internet?'

Following Conor's YouTube success, and particularly due to his chat with Ne-Yo, it wasn't long before a frenzy to sign the latest hot stuff on the music scene ensued.

At 17, Conor eventually signed to EMI Parlophone and immediately began work on his debut album, *Contrast*: 'I signed with EMI – I had to have my dad's signature underneath mine because I was only 17.'

Telling Ne-Yo that he was turning him down wasn't easy, but the music superstar took it well, with Conor revealing: 'I started working on the first album. There was no grudges, he understood and told me he still wanted to work with me.'

Ne-Yo supplied a song that he wrote for Conor's debut album, entitled 'Turn Around'. Conor recorded the whole song, and then Ne-Yo told his young protégé that he needed to be on the song – prompting much delight.

Working on the album was something new for Conor. He told *TheArtsDesk*: 'Definitely a weird transition as I was so used to singing other people's songs. When it came to writing original material I wasn't even sure what direction I wanted to go in. The first year of me being signed was experimenting in the studio, finding out what sort of artist I wanted to be. I was only 17 when I signed so I was growing up while finding my sound.'

He told *ilikemusic*: 'When I was doing the covers it was apparent that people from all over the world were watching them. When you looked at the demographics of where the views were coming from it was in England, the US, Germany, Australia – all over the place. The label realised that it had to be an international thing, and for me, I want to be an internationally successful artist. I want to be able to tour in all of those countries. World domination! You know, just casually running the world! Haha.'

Unbeknown to Conor was the fact that a songwriting team was keeping a close eye on him, even before he signed to EMI. John Shave from Invisible Men revealed: 'Conor was a name we kept hearing from various people that we had met. Eventfully a friend of ours showed it [his work] to us. I think all three of us had the same reaction. We were blown away by his tone. He has this amazing vocal tone. I think the first song we saw him do was "Use Somebody" by Kings of Leon. It was really clever what he was trying to do. He was showing off his voice in completely his own style and had done his own really cool arrangement of the track. And right away we were like, who is this guy? We need to meet him. And then it was a complete coincidence actually, because a week later than that he happened to be in this building meeting our manager. And he walked in, and we were like, "That's Conor Maynard". It was kind of like he was a celebrity already to us. We started hanging out with him. He wasn't signed at this point. We actually just loved having him around – he was just a really great laugh. He's just got this insane sense of humour. Back in those days we'd do a little bit of writing, but there was no pressure. It was just really organic.'

Conor recorded a demo called 'Fire' – an uptempo dance track, about setting the world on fire and losing yourself in the moment. His first live show was at the Haunt in Brighton, a dark, dingy club with a small stage with little space for him to move about in.

He said: 'I remember stepping out and I was kind of wandering about, thinking, what am I going to say? I think a lot of my friends noticed I was pretty nervous doing my first ever show. I've always been good interacting with my audiences. I used to do it on my covers, being the idiot that I am. It just made me excited going to all these different places I had never been to and meeting more crazy Mayniacs all over the world.'

However, he knew that he had to be switched on, as everything was getting very serious now. There was little room for error, but luckily he knew this. He told *Bizarre*: 'I started with a cheap webcam in my room, now I'm signed. The pressure's on to write songs that will be as good as the ones I've covered online.'

He was hailed as one to watch when, in 2012, he won MTV's Brand New For 2012. It was a stunning success and forcibly marked him as a future pop star. At this point, he hadn't released any original material, and was up against some formidable competition, among them Delilah, Michael Kiwanuka, Lana Del Rey and Lianne La Havas.

Conor spoke to MTV after he received his nomination: 'When I heard I was nominated for MTV's Brand New For 2012, it was just a massive shock. Ever since I was little I have been watching MTV and it was one of those dreams, like, "Ah wow, imagine if one day I was on it". It really gives you a big boost in confidence and it's a really cool feeling.'

After receiving a staggering 45 per cent of the vote, he was crowned the winner on 31 January. He said: 'When I was first announced to be in the Top 10, and I saw the other names, obviously Lana Del Ray, I was like, "Okay, number two guys, we're going for number two." Yeah, it was crazy to go on and win that with the massive names already in the line-up. Hearing that I had won was cool enough, but hearing that I had taken pretty much half the votes was amazing. I was definitely thankful to everyone who voted.'

Conor joked, 'My mum had gone right in there, with 20 votes a day. She almost lost her job!'

Credit for his victory must go to his Facebook army, though. Speaking at the event, he said, 'It's going crazy right now. I think in terms of statistics it's mad. I think I've just reached 161,000 likes. I think I'm the most liked artist on Facebook that hasn't released anything yet, ever, in the UK.'

MTV announced his victory, hailing: 'We're delighted to announce that Brighton boy Conor Maynard has been crowned the winner of MTV's Brand New For 2012. Maynard scored an incredible 45 per cent of viewers' votes in our annual search for the very best in new music, beating competition from hotly tipped acts including Lana Del Rey, Charli XCX and King Charles.'

Of his win, Conor said: 'It's such an amazing feeling winning MTV's Brand New For 2012. I can't thank the fans and viewers enough for voting, and MTV for selecting me in the first place! Hope this is the first success of many to come!'

For him, it was a huge foot in the door. The MTV Brand New was not just any music competition; it is regarded with great esteem and previous acts that have been identified by MTV Brand New include Lady Gaga, Ke$ha, Jessie J and Tinie Tempah, as well as Justin Bieber. It showed he was in very good company indeed. Unsurprisingly Conor took it very seriously. Prior to his appearance, he spent hours with his stylists and vocal coach.

Wearing a black leather jacket and a black and white striped top, he headed for the event as confident as he could be. However, there was a potential pitfall in the shape of the dreaded red carpet. Not only would he have to perform to an audience, he would also have to meet the press and pose for photos. This was a relatively new experience for Conor as he awkwardly answered questions from journalists, his nerves visible and his confidence shaky. 'I haven't tripped over anything yet,' sighed Conor to a journalist from the *Mirror*, smiling as he began to transform into the part. Suddenly, he began to utter new, confident sound bites. Whereas previously they stumbled hazily out, now they sprung with machine-gun efficiency – 'With me, because I switched it up so much, I made it my own song and really drew people's attention on YouTube' and 'When you look at me, you wouldn't expect the voice to come out.'

Soon afterwards, he admitted: 'There were some pretty tough questions in there.'

It was a hugely contested event, with more than 150,000 votes counted. When the winner was announced by MTV, Conor was dubbed a possible contender for the 'world's next big teen star'. In second place came King Charles, an eclectic musician who draws on a number of diverse influences, including glam rock, hip-hop, country and Afro Beat. Pop sensation Lana Del Rey was in third place, while grime stars Clement Marfo & The Frontline were fourth; RnB star Angel rounded out the top five. With her own compositions played on a piano, 20-year-old Delilah was in sixth place, while pop singer Charli XCX, rock star Michael Kiwanuka, Lianne La Havas and Context (a star who blends dub step and hip-hop) made up the Top 10.

Conor told *hitthefloor*: 'It made me really

excited to get going. I obviously hadn't released anything yet and it was really early. We were just starting to go and it gave us a really good push. It started off a big buzz with the media.'

He was working on the set of his video shoot when he discovered that he had won the award. It meant that that he had to keep the celebrations under wraps as he finished the video. He joked: 'There were a lot of pretty ladies around the video shoot to keep me happy anyway. It was all good.'

Of his win, he said: 'I think it was kind of the first step in taking off. I mean, before that I was already working on my first album and being told I was in that list, that was a big enough honour anyway. I always watched it growing up thinking and imagining if I was on MTV one day, and then to be on that list was absolutely crazy. I saw Lana Del Rey on it and I thought I was gonna be number two but no, it came to the point where I was number one and I was told that I'd taken 45 per cent of the votes, and that was amazing. I was so excited to get it.'

He added: 'I was the only person on that list who hadn't released an official original track and I was up against people like Lana Del Rey. MTV were playing an advert with me on it and they had to use a bad-quality YouTube video of me in my room with a microphone. But I got all these votes and ended up in first place. It was crazy and shows how lucky I am to have a big online following.'

He ended up meeting Lana once again, but refused to gloat: 'No! Literally on my way back from the EMAs, Lana Del Rey sat directly behind me on the flight, but I didn't turn around and tell her that. I think it might have been a bit rude. She probably would have just said "Who are you?"'

He revealed: 'Last year I won MTV's Brand New award – that's what transformed me from someone who could walk around like a normal person to the craziness that I experience now. I was given these trainers as a present for winning – I've never worn them because I want to keep them pristine. After that award, I started getting stopped in the street. Now it's at the stage where I've had to move out of my old flat because my fans knew where I lived and were waiting for me then my phone number got out, and I woke up and I had hundreds of missed calls overnight.'

He had simple ambitions, stating: 'I think I am mainly looking forward to reaching the success that I have worked so hard to get to, releasing the singles, releasing the albums, seeing and hearing my singles on the TV and radio, that's my goal in terms of what I am really aiming to achieve.

Turning on the radio one day not expecting your tune to be playing but you hear it randomly, or walking into a shop and you just hear your track playing in the background. I think that's the success I really want to reach and hopefully look forward to.'

The winner of the MTV Brand New For 2013 was Ebony Day. Not only did she share similarities with Conor Maynard, thanks to becoming prominent uploading songs on YouTube, they also had a duet on the social site.

Their 2011 take on Chris Brown's 'Next to You' has attracted over 11 million views on YouTube.

Despite working together, Ebony and Conor only met face-to-face at the MTV London show in January 2013.

Ebony said about their eventual meeting to MTV: 'We went up to the dressing room just before he went onstage so I just said hello. It was nice to see him because I've never actually met him before, so it was cool to see how he has gone from YouTube and now hopefully I'll do the same type of journey.'

The 19-year-old said about her plans for her upcoming single: 'The single is going to be pop music... quite acoustic-y. I don't want to go too far away from what I've done on YouTube so it will still like have an acoustic edge to it but a little bit different.'

She beat off other acts for the victory, including the hotly tipped Garbrielle Aplin and Haim – and she was the only act not to be signed by a major label.

She was dubbed the female Conor Maynard after notching up 19 million views on YouTube. Her victory was all the more impressive after she nabbed 40 per cent of votes despite very little press coverage. But her fans, just like's Conor's Mayniacs, are a loyal bunch and were desperate to show their support for the singer.

She added about the victory: 'I'm so overwhelmed that my fans have made this win possible for me! It's all down to their ongoing support and hard work that I have won MTV's Brand New For 2013 and I can't thank them enough. This is a dream come true for me, I've never been happier.'

She added about celebrating her Brand New For 2013 win: 'I'll probably celebrate by going to the cinema or something! I've got some jelly in the other room so I'll probably eat some jelly…!'

CHAPTER FOUR

CAN'T SAY NO TO POP SUCCESS

With an MTV victory under his belt, it was now on to the more serious stuff.

Conor had made an impact with the covers, but now he had to show that he could carry on the momentum with something original. And there was further hype to maintain following his stunning MTV Brand New victory. In the studio he had found himself writing songs with other songwriting partners in the hope of channelling the passion from his covers into new material.

While Conor was being tipped for chart glory, however it didn't necessarily guarantee success.

The road to music's elite is paved with the dashed dreams of wannabe superstars who have failed to live up to their potential. Hype and success don't necessarily go hand in hand, and with music-buying audiences increasingly cynical about the latest hot new thing, it's only right that Conor was being judged, not by the bluster from the music press and TV but by his own talents.

Luckily, he is not someone who was plucked from a talent show and thrown into a situation where he would have to rely on other people to conjure up songs and a musical direction to take. Rooted in an urban sound, thanks to the records his parents listened to and the videos he tried to emulate on YouTube, he knew exactly what sort of performer he wanted to become. While comparisons with Justin Bieber were mooted when he first burst onto the scene, the artists he admired were less of the cutesy pop attributed to Bieber's earlier work; more artists with a harder, urban-edged sound such as Drake and Chris Brown.

Talking to *The Edge* about the comparisons, he said: 'Erm, you know it does get a bit old, and sometimes it's a bit like, "Right, okay, I get it, guys". But I think it's just one of those things where people see that we're both young, we both came through YouTube and therefore I have to be him. Where it's a bit like, "No!" because you look back at it when Chris Brown and Usher and Ne-Yo were big, they could easily be compared to each other but they still had their own sound and they were still original in their own way. I think for me sometimes it's like, "Yeah, okay," there can be a lot of similarities between artists but you're not trying to BE them! I think for me, obviously I'm British, I'm slightly older than him [Bieber], I think it's got more of an edgy sound to it, I think it's just a different thing. I think the more people that have heard the album, the more they start to realise that it's not what they think it is. So for me one of the main reasons I named the album *Contrast* is because it felt like the album itself is a contrast to what everyone seemed to be expecting, they were obviously expecting this young poppy album and it really wasn't that.'

But he wasn't content with spending all his time in the recording studio. In fact he refused to take his MTV win lightly: one option would have been to coast on the victory which, combined with the following he had from his internet cover songs, would have been enough to support a rushed-through effort. However, Conor realised that not only would the record have to be of a high quality, he must also ensure that he could play to an audience. Despite the self-deprecating humour and quick wit apparent in the videos that he posted, he still needed to prove he could cut it live on stage.

With expectations high for this young talent, he began touring to show exactly why he had won the MTV contest and that he could live outside the world of YouTube. He needed to perfect his stage presence to ensure he was the complete package, not just a social media curio item.

Before the release of his debut song, he said: 'I still feel like I've got a long way to go. Things have got really exciting already but this is something I've always wanted to do, so I want to work hard at this.'

Being out in front of a crowd was a new thing for the young singer who was more accustomed to belting out songs in the school canteen than performing in front of large audiences – some already in love with the cocky upstart, others eager to see if he delivered on the hype. In February 2012, he told *PyroMag*: 'For me, starting the live shows was kind of crazy. It was definitely nerve-wracking because I did my first show the other week in my hometown of Brighton, so I knew a lot of people at the gig personally. It was nerve-wracking in the sense that I was presenting my own original material that no one had ever heard before, so obviously you are a bit worried whether or not people are going to like it.

'However, the response was really cool. I performed the songs with talking gaps, probably making an idiot out of myself, like I do on YouTube because I wanted to show that side of me is still there, but the music is just kind of different and my own now.'

He added to *worksopguardian.co.uk*: 'I'll be playing some un-heard tracks as well as a few familiar ones. I've been getting more experience on stage with some recent performances so I'm hoping this tour will be a crazy experience for everyone who comes along.'

The tour kicked off in Bristol on 20 April.

Conor told *hitthefloor.co.uk* about the ticket sales, which started off at £10: 'It's so funny, right, because we were selling them [the tickets] on a sales website, and they were being advertised on another website, where they were reselling them, I suppose. I guess someone had bought them and they're reselling them. And they were being advertised, Coldplay, like £30, Drake, £40, One Direction, £50, Conor Maynard, £70. I was like double the price of Coldplay and Drake. It makes me look real good, doesn't it?'

He told *Confront Magazine*: 'It's amazing. I'll

never forget when I did one of my first shows and the fans were singing, "HOUSTON, I THINK WE GOT A PROBLEM!" back at me. It was just crazy. I mean, to think that only a few months before I was in the studio messing around with those lyrics whilst writing them. Now fans have taken the time to learn them and sing them back at me!'

As the shows went on, his confidence began to blossom and very soon a true music performer was in evidence. He added: 'I feel like performing is probably one of my favourite parts of being an artist and kind of like, vibing off the audience and the energy when you're performing. Drawing them in when you do a slow song and making them jump around when you're doing a crazy song; I think it's a really cool vibe. I also did one in Brighton, where I'm from – that was the first show that my parents came to that was my own so that was pretty special.'

Then talking about his pre-show ritual to *TheYorker.co.uk*, he said: 'I do a lot of vocal exercises and warm-ups. That's really my manager shouting at me to do them because they are literally the most embarrassing things to do. I also always pace a lot, so I can think of exactly what I have to do and then I get the band in to hype each other up by punching each other in the face. Nah,

I'm just kidding! We just all get each other excited and do a big hands in the middle and shout.'

He added to the *Telegraph*: 'I don't like to see the crowd before I go onstage. I do warm-ups: I steam my vocal cords. I've got this weird thing that looks like a teapot that you put boiling water in and inhale the vapour. Right before the gig I pace up and down to get myself hyped up.'

And he was certainly a hit with the ladies, telling *Yahoo! OMG!*: 'Underwear is one of the things that is thrown on to the stage when I'm performing. Another thing is Maoam [Haribos sweets]. Me and my band sneakily tweeted our favourite sweets before we went on tour. I annoyingly chose a sweet that really hurts when it hits you in the face. I got hit by a scarf too. It doesn't sound very manly, but it actually hurt – they scrunched it up very small.'

With his live show persona being perfected, he had to hope he had done enough and whetted the fans' appetites for his singles.

The first song was to be 'Can't Say No', the lead single of his debut album *Contrast*. Conor and his team would dance in the studio, listening to the catchy beat, convinced they had a hit on their hands. Conor himself wrote the track with songwriting trio, The Invisible Men. They comprise of Jon Shave (of famous production team Xenomania) and rock band Orson stars Jason Pebworth and George Astasio.

The Invisible Men have been responsible for several of the greatest pop hits over the last few years, including 'Do It Like A Dude' from Jessie J and Rita Ora's 'Hot Right Now'. Based in London, they were named one of *Music Week*'s Top Songwriters in a chart compiled in 2011. They wrote Conor's first two songs, and the young singer was delighted with their input.

He told *The Arts Desk*: 'I definitely liked stuff they'd done in the past. When I first started the album, I much preferred working with people I felt comfortable with and The Invisible Men were the first producers who really understood what music I wanted to make. They were really helpful and I connected with them really quickly, worked on a lot of cuts that eventually made the album.'

The debut song's origins began with a beat – a simple but effective beat that Jon Shave felt could be the beginning of a great pop song. Even when they weren't officially signed to work with him, they had been helping Conor on tracks.

Jon said: 'We were playing this crazy-sounding beat, thinking this would be amazing for Conor if we could get a song to go with it. I think it was the third day into those sessions, and he just kept singing, "Houston, I think we've got a problem." And it was such a random line. He said: "I really like this line, guys." And we were like, okay, let's do it.'

The memorable line about Houston was the starting lyric of the song, and it was Conor's first big idea when coming up with the tongue-in-cheek track. He said: 'It's completely random for me. Things just pop into my head. It's just one of those things where sometimes you have a moment where you're suddenly inspired by something, or you have a sudden idea and it just flows out of you. Other times, you really don't know what to write about and it doesn't go too smoothly. But either way, I think it's just random. When I was writing "Can't Say No", the only idea I had in my head to start with was the whole, "Houston, I think we got a problem". So, we put that before the chorus and then we thought, "Okay, how are we going to link this into an actual song? What can we say for the rest of it?" And I was thinking of how people are always saying, "Oh, you must have a lot of girls now," and it was like, "Okay, I'm going to play on that. Oh, there's just so many girls I just can't say no."'

He added: 'I was in the studio with The Invisible

Men and Sophie Stern when I first heard the backing track, and I instantly loved it, and knew I wanted to write a crazy party track over it! The only idea I had in my head at first was the line "Houston, I think we got a problem" as I wanted that to be the part that everyone knows and everyone sings along to. After that we wrote the "girls, girls, girls" chorus and tied it all together. The song was definitely meant to be taken more tongue-in-cheek, not taken too seriously; it was just a fun idea that would get people dancing and singing along! I wasn't trying to say that no matter where I go, girls just jump on me. I wish that was the case, haha!'

The other writers for the song were Sophie Stern, Jon Mills, Joe Dyer and Kurtis McKenzie. Conor said: 'I really enjoy being able to write my own music. I wrote eight of the 12 tracks on the album. It is one of the things you can never be forced to do. You have to have an idea – it just comes naturally without any warning! For me, I have to believe what I am singing about, and to know exactly what I'm singing about, some of it is about past experiences, past relationships. I'm a 19-year-old guy – I like to party and have fun, and so when I write, I am my own audience.'

The number of writers needed for what is

essentially a party song might seem high, but it was essential to get this right. In an industry where first appearances must be pretty much perfect, nothing could be left to chance.

He added: 'I had time to chill with The Invisible Men. We sat around for a couple of weeks, taking our time. It's how I think I work best generally, though sometimes what you can get in 15 minutes is incredible. It's like the stars were aligned with that tune – the second I heard it, I loved it.'

Despite the subject manner and his confident delivery, Conor possessed a rare gift in that it didn't come across as arrogance, more a cheeky boy trying to have a bit of fun. He later admitted in an interview: 'Some people heard that and thought, "Oh you must be a dick, saying you get girls all the time." But it's just a party record and a bit of fun. I wasn't literally saying that, because it really wasn't the case at the time.'

He also added in an interview to *Pyromag*: 'Yeah the single "Can't Say No" was produced by The Invisible Men, who have also produced stuff for Jessie J, like "Do It Like A Dude". When writing this track, we just kind of had this fun vibe going on in the studio. It's a catchy song that's not really meant to be taken seriously because in it I'm talking about being able to get any girl I want, so you can't really take the track seriously. It's a jokey song that people can just sing along to.'

The video was released on 1 March 2012 and was quickly lapped up by music TV channels. The music press and fans of Conor also seemed to be pleased with the debut effort and Conor and his management team breathed a sigh of relief following the positive response.

Conor said: 'A lot of artists that I meet definitely have had advice and it's normally the same thing: it's all about enjoying yourself. They always ask me, "Are you enjoying it? Are you enjoying yourself?" Because a lot of people look at the music industry and think it's all glitz and glamour, and really it isn't. There are a lot of hardships. You have to go through a lot of difficult situations, so make sure you're enjoying yourself. Make sure, you know, when you're performing and in the studio, you're having as much fun as possible because, you know, if you're not enjoying yourself, then it's going to become a struggle. It's going to become a bit of a massive drag.'

As mentioned earlier, comparisons with Justin Bieber continued to surface, with each interview bringing Bieber up. However, as he had done several times before, Conor tried to downplay the similarities: 'Comparisons just naturally come early in a musician's career. People are trying to guess who you're trying to be like, what your sound is trying to be. I'd much rather people just listen to the music and make their own opinions, make their own comparisons for themselves. You know, I'm not trying to be the next anyone; I'm trying to be the first Conor Maynard. I'm just doing me and I know that that is different. I suppose sometimes it makes you think, "Well, it's kind of difficult because if people out there don't like Justin Bieber, they're not going to listen to me because they think it's the same thing when really it isn't." So I think that's the only kind of downside of it, but at the same time, he's one of the biggest artists in the world right now, and being compared to him isn't, I suppose, probably a bad thing.'

The video of 'Can't Say No' was directed by Rohan Blair-Mangat, who had recently enjoyed success at the helm of DJ Fresh and Rita Ora's pop promo 'Hot Right Now'. Producers included Tom Knight and Tom Birmingham while the video was made by production company Rokkit.

The 3m 15s video was shot in one day in east London and saw young Conor singing, aptly, in his bedroom before hitting the streets of London, and then a night club, where he enjoys himself dancing around a group of girls.

While shooting his first video he was instantly aware of pop-star perks. He told *FirstNews.co.uk*: 'My brother came to my first ever video shoot and he's actually in the video for "Can't Say No". For me, that's pretty mad. We were both standing there, just looking around this huge house that we were shooting this party in, all the people there, and I was just like, "This is all here for me? This is all here for the song that I wrote?" There were so many people, nearly 200!'

Jack was also expected to be in the follow-up track – 'Vegas Girl'. But, being under 18, it was decided that he would have to miss shooting the party track as he would have been too young for the then planned shoot in Sin City. However, seeing as it is illegal to drink under the age of 21, even Conor had to change his plans and shoot elsewhere.

Rohan Blair-Mangat told this author: 'I was approached by the video commissioner of EMI; when he approached me, I had just done the video for Rita Ora and DJ Fresh. He was looking for the same tone for Conor Maynard, and he asked me to come up with an idea. He gave me a brief, which told me how they wanted to market him and the things Conor came up with. I had to come up with an idea from the guidelines that they laid out.

'With a new artist and a debut video it's

especially important to get it right because you're setting the tone for the future. If it isn't right, it could cause a lot of trouble down the line. With Conor they played me the song, and a few others he was working on at the time. And they just directed me to his YouTube channel, which is where he got noticed in the first place. I just watched his videos and saw what kind of guy he was like. The bedroom scene at the beginning was something that they were quite keen on at the beginning, to show where he came from.

'With this video it's not like the later ones that he did, where it's almost like a big US pop video: this was a transitional video. He was self-taught at that point, which was really admirable. One of the things that was quite important was not going too far with the production; let's not run before we can walk. You've got to build it slowly and authentically. You can see over the four videos how he has grown; the fans go along with it.

'I had some other ideas for the video but was a bit cautious about making a Justin Timberlake-like video. I just remember thinking that the temptation is to show these stars with a lifestyle that you want to fulfil, to sell something that is larger than life. But he was only about 19 or something at that time, so it couldn't be something too crazy that will have people questioning his world and what he does; it has to be honest. I remember going through my initial ideas thinking that it could work but perhaps it's too soon.'

Given that it was Conor's first ever music video, he must have felt the pressure on him. But Rohan insisted that the youngster was in the right frame of mind from the start. 'I really enjoyed working with him,' he said. 'I met him a couple of times, I think, before the shoot. I went to a rehearsal that he was doing and we went out for lunch to break the ice, I guess. I was really surprised at how switched on he was. I don't mean switched on like, in a horrible way: he's really intelligent and he knows what he wants. I guess it comes from those videos that he did. He knows what image he wants and how he wants to appear. Like any first-time big budget music video artist, he needed a bit of direction, but it would only be for the camera.

'He used to pick the songs that he wanted to, so he knows the kind of artists that he wants to be.

'The vibe on the set was a balance. It was quite easy-going in the sense of people enjoying themselves but at the same time you always feel a bit of pressure when it's a first-time singer making a video – it's kind of make or break. If the video doesn't do what it sets out to do then it can be a crutch for an artist. It was quite an ambitious idea for what it was. It might not seem like it, but to think, this is a first single and it was shot in one day.

'All those extras for the party scene, then you've got the scene outside and you've got his room as well. It's a lot to shoot in one day, and to do it well. Conor is one of those big artists so the video has to have lots of beautiful shots. So you would spend a lot of time on things like that. I guess the time frame being tight can amp the feeling of pressure but it wasn't that bad, to be fair. It was a lot of fun and I look back fondly on it, to be honest.'

Talking about the house video shoot, Rohan continued: 'Those kinds of shoots have the highs and lows. During the take, there's lot of high energy and everyone is having fun. But it's the dead time in between when you're checking it back or you're moving people about and reset all the angles and check the lights; it's hard to motivate so many extras. At first everyone is really excited, but after a few hours you have to bring them back. One thing Conor is really good at, and that day was a perfect example. I really like him because he's very genuine. He wasn't in his own area or just doing his own thing; if someone wanted to talk to him he would talk to people and have fun with them. He's just a young kid enjoying himself. He wasn't being a diva or being a superstar, and I think that helped bring the crowd along. You're like, "Oh, this guy is very approachable, I feel a part of it". It creates this energy, which I think is good.'

The video was a hit with the fans and it was played constantly on many of the music channels.

'The reaction was very positive,' said Rohan. 'I didn't know what to expect with a music video like that, or what it would do. I think it's done what it set out to do, and I think it has done well. It's done pretty well.'

Conor was clearly pleased with his debut, telling the *Independent*: 'I didn't want to go with something too poppy for the single. My roots are in rap and harder urban pop. I did exactly what I wanted to do.'

The critics seemed equally pleased, with many praising the effort. *Digital Spy* said about the song: '"Can't Say No" is more than likely to set the Brighton-born lad down a similar path [as Justin Bieber]. "Some girls are naughty, some girls are sweet/One thing they got in common, they all got a hold on me," he croons over buzzing bass and crisp beats, before things tumble into an ear-grabbing chorus bouncier than an inflatable castle.

In fact, the final result is much the same; it's playful, fun and immediately leaves you wanting another go.'

CBBC *Newsround* insisted the song was one that would grow, adding: '"Can't Say No" is a confident and laid-back debut from the teenager, who shows off his soulful voice against a mid-tempo backdrop of electronic beats and booms.

'It's only his first single and he's already purring about how he can't say no to girls – we can tell he's trying to appeal to the females!'

The *Bradford Student* was less impressed, writing: 'We're in the very early stages of Maynard's career, so I won't write him off entirely, and I can see how maybe I am a little out of the target audience of Maynard's work, who is currently being compared with Justin Bieber. At the moment, I would actually go to say Bieber is a better musician, even if he is like a twelve-year-old! Maynard is still just a little too new, despite being around since 2008 (on YouTube). I'm sure the guy has potential to become a big star, with the likes of Olly Murs or Rizzle Kicks, but right now I would say he still needs some fine-tuning before he becomes commercial.

'Would I suggest you go out and purchase "Can't Say No"? Probably not. I would suggest you look it up online, however, as Maynard has the potential to go far in later life.'

However, *BBM Live* wrote: 'The BBM opinion of this track "Can't Say No" is that although the lyrics are pretty teeny bopper and dripping in glucose the actual backing track is pretty damn good and is just waiting to be remixed!'

Meanwhile, *Seventeen.com* raved: 'The British Invasion continues! UK sensation Conor Maynard just released the music video for his single "Can't Say No". The song harkens back a fun blend of early Justin Timberlake with a bit of Usher's soulful sound mixed in. He looks and sounds like the UK's answer to *Seventeen* cover star Justin Bieber so be aware that you'll be singing "girls, girls, girls, I just can't say no" for hours as you replay the song and share it with your friends.'

Maximum Pop were also impressed, commenting: 'Rather than capitalise on that knicker-twisting voice with an overblown, tuned-up ballad, Conor's laid-back debut is a hypnotic, slutty club beat production piece with a Timberlake vocal, an infectious "girls, girls, girls" refrain and the "Houston, I think we've got a problem" line that is in approximately 12 per cent of pop hits released in the last five years. It's cooler and more exciting then you'd expect, and probably a lot filthier than your mum would like.'

But the song didn't just impress the majority of critics. Conor's single also received endorsement from two big pop stars – Aussie pop princess Kylie Minogue, who tweeted to Conor: 'Can't Say No Go Go Go!!!!' and Lily Allen, who tweeted, 'Houston..i think we got a problem' – referencing the song's lyrics.

He reciprocated later in 2012, by saying: 'Everyone make sure you've got the beautiful @KylieMinogue's new album 'The Abbey Road Sessions' here – http://smarturl.it/KylieAbbeyRd!!!'

In a bid to ensure chart glory, no stone was left unturned as his management team tried to drum up as much interest as they could for their new star, embarking on a promotional blitz in a bid to score a number one. Conor said: 'It would feel insane. I was doing my radio tour and meeting a lot of DJs across the country, and they were like, "Come on, it's going to be number one" and I was like, "Whaaaat! So much competition!" But for me, I'm excited about it; I'll take it as it comes. I look at other artists like Ed Sheeran, Justin Bieber – massive artists who have never had a number one in the UK.'

His debut single was released in the UK on 29

April 2012. It debuted at number two in the UK Singles Chart selling nearly 75,000 copies. When informed by Radio 1, Conor remarked: 'Number two – I'm cool man. Hang up, I'm done – aw man, I'm so excited!'

While it never landed the top spot, Conor was still on Cloud Nine after making such an instant impact, telling the *Independent*: 'It's pretty amazing for the single to go in so high. I'm still figuring out how all this works.'

He added in an interview to the *Liverpool Echo*: 'It's pretty nuts. When I went to number two I had a little celebration in Brighton with my mates. Everything that has happened so far has been amazing, but I'm not about to take my eye off the ball. Right now, I'm getting ready for the next step because I don't want to trip myself up. This is the most exciting thing to happen to me, and I don't want it to stop.'

In Ireland, it peaked at number 13, while the song rose to number three in the Scottish charts.

Again, not one to rest his laurels, Conor was soon hard at work on the follow-up single and the album. He said: 'Very busy, getting up really early, which is great! There's obviously a level of commitment that's expected from you being a singer and you've got to give 110 per cent

Conor blasts onto
the pop scene with
his first album
Contrast, which
debuts at number 1.
© *Getty Images*

Everyone wants a piece of Conor as he hits television screens and red carpets worldwide.

Above left: Conor strikes a pose on the red carpet before performing at *T4 On the Beach* in 2012.
© Getty Images

Above right: Sending girls crazy on *New.Music.Live*, a television show in Canada.
© Getty Images

Below: Being grilled during an interview in Toronto, Canada.
© Rex Features

onor is adored by fans all over the world. Here he takes time to greet a mass of
lmirers in New York.

Conor doing what he does best: performing!

Above: Sharing the stage with American superstar and mentor Ne-Yo, who first spotted Conor singing on YouTube.

© Rex Featur

Below: From Brighton to the bright lights, Conor takes centre stage in Canada t sing his best-loved hits.

© Getty Imag

Conor is often spotted mingling with celebrity pals.

Posing alongside Harry Styles, one-fifth of hugely successful boy band One Direction.

© Dave M. Bennett/Getty Images

bove left: Conor getting up close and personal with fellow pop star Rita Ora on night out at London's exclusive VIP club Mahiki. © *Dave M. Bennett/Getty Images*

bove right: Looking dapper, Conor escorts Eliza Doolittle to a ball in Battersea, ondon. © *Getty Images*

elow: Partying with cast members of Geordie Shore and Jedward backstage at ne MTV EMA's in Frankfurt, Germany, 2012. © *Getty Images*

Conor often jets off to showcase his music around the world!

Above: Tourist Conor heads across the pond to visit New York's famous Empire State Building.

© Getty Image

Below: Conor soaking up the sights in Milan, Italy.

© Getty Image

otherwise someone else will take that from you. But for me, it's cool. It goes from interviews to being in the studio to getting on a plane, going to some random corner of the world that I've never been to before, meeting all different fans – "Mayniacs", as they're called.'

Talking about media pressure, he remarked: 'It is kind of exhausting, but it is early days and it's going to get worse, the bigger it gets. But it's cool. Some artists get every single press person in one room at the same time so they can answer all their questions and tell them to go away, but I'm not big enough or enough of a diva to do that! I do answer the same questions lots of times, but I try to throw something new in there for each person!'

Days after his UK single chart success, Conor treated the fans who pre-ordered the record *Contrast* to a free download of his upcoming album track 'Drowning'. He said: 'What a lot of people don't know is that it's not all glitz and glamour, there's a lot of pressure on you. There's a thousand other people who want it as well, and would easily take it from you within a second if they had the chance. It is kind of difficult sometimes but coming back home takes the weight off my shoulders.'

The ambitious young star was not just set on

dominating the British charts. Conor had one eye on conquering the American charts following his UK triumph, especially after he was in the US at the same time as One Direction topped the charts stateside. He said: 'There's a big hype on British talent right now; I kept thinking this is a really good time for me. All eyes are on the UK. They are waiting for the next new British talent and I want to capitalise on that.'

He added to *Glamour*: 'I don't really know what it is – there's just been a sudden surge of UK talent recently. I don't know whether it's luck or fate, or whether something has actually happened. One theory I've got is that it was the one series of the UK *X Factor* that they had over in the States, and they didn't have that before. They had *American Idol*, but it got a bit old. And it was that one series where it was One Direction, Cher Lloyd. And I think for that period of time there were a lot of eyes on British talent. And obviously there was Adele – she's a worldwide superstar. Now The Wanted, and now Ed Sheeran – I just think it's a really good time.'

Around this time, he became good friends with One Direction after meeting them on the pop star touring circuit. Despite their clean-cut image the boy band are something of a group of party animals. Conor, who isn't much of a drinker, once threw up and collapsed in a garden after partying with his new pals. He told the *Sunday Mirror*: 'There was one time I got so drunk I was throwing up and collapsed in someone's garden. That's only happened once. I think Niall [Horan] could out-drink every single one of us put together. It's the Irish, it's in their genes. At V Festival, Niall was drunk-singing my songs to me. I love him.'

However, not all the One Direction boys were in the Team Conor camp.

Zayn Malik took to Twitter to announce that he preferred listening to Justin Bieber rather than Conor Maynard after he was asked by a fan. He wrote: 'Nah Biebers better like :) sorry gotta stay loyal ! :)'

Meanwhile, still flushed with the success of his debut, Conor performed 'Can't Say No' at the TRL Awards in Italy in March. A month later, he also performed the hit song at the Capital Summertime Ball, wowing 80,000 music goers.

In April 2012, a performance at Dingwalls in Camden saw him attract several celebrity fans. Lily Allen, Radio 1 DJ Nick Grimshaw and Lily's TV presenter pal Miquita Oliver gave him the celebrity seal of approval by attending his show. Before the event Lily became a self-confessed Mayniac, excitingly tweeting music website *Popjustice* to ask: '@Popjustice are you going to see Conor Maynard later?'

To which they replied: '@MrsLRCooper Sadly I'm in f***** Wales but throw some underwear for me if you're going'.

Lily tweeted back happily: '@Popjustice will dooooooo #mayniacs' and also uploaded a picture of her concert ticket, tweeting 'Big Gig'. She was pictured wearing a white T-shirt, with the word 'Mayniac' printed on it. She was also heard joking to a bouncer before heading into the gig: 'Are there actually any adults in there?'

Conor told *Bang Showbiz*: 'It was amazing to know Lily Allen came along to one of my first shows in London, and she even bought her own ticket, which was the best part. I only found out on the day, so I was crazy.'

He also added to the *Daily Star*: 'I hear she's back in the studio – I would love to work with her. It's a really cool feeling when artists I'm inspired by say they like my music as well. We're on the same label, it would have to be the right song but I could never say no to that.'

It was around this time that he had finished work on the album, telling the newspaper: 'This week the album was mixed and I heard it complete for the first time. Working with all those talented people was amazing and also an honour. I was in the studio last night with Ne-Yo and David Guetta. It was surreal, listening to the track Ne-Yo did with David there.'

Conor's stock continued to rise, and just when it looked as if it couldn't get any better, he won Best Newcomer at the Nordoff Robbins O2 Silver Clef Awards at the London Hilton on 12 June 2012. The announcement read: 'Both Emeli [Sandé] and Conor have catapulted into the limelight this year, so it is no surprise that they are being congratulated for their vast achievements together joining Andrew Lloyd Webber, Jessie J, Michael Bublé and Laura Wright, who have already been announced this year.'

Conor said: 'This is an honour for me. To win such a prestigious award so early on in my career, I couldn't have hoped for more. It's been such a mad year so far, and winning the TAG Best Newcomer Award at the O2 Silver Clef lunch is wonderful. The Awards have celebrated some of the most iconic artists in the last 40 years, and it is incredible to be anywhere near that list. It feels really great just to be a part of it with the TAG Newcomer Award and it's crazy to think that this time last year it was Tinie Tempah picking up this

Award. I'm really looking forward to it and can't thank Nordoff Robbins enough.'

And he prepared for it rock-star style, turning up in a helicopter. Before the event, he said: 'I'm getting Best Newcomer, which is a cool thing. It's so early in my career, but it's something I'll always remember. I've got a mad day. I'm doing a surprise appearance, then going to Leeds for a performance and then taking a helicopter back again.'

Afterwards, he added to *FirstNews.co.uk*: 'It was mad. I actually hated the helicopter, if I'm honest, though. Oh my goodness, it was the worst experience of my life. It's not even scary – it's just horrible! And your stomach's going urgh! It makes you feel so sick. I'll take my travel sickness pills next time before I go.' Despite this, he described the win as an 'amazing feeling'.

He also showcased his talents at the BBC Live Lounge in late 2012, singing a cover of Nicki Minaj's 'Starships'. The heartfelt ballad won him new fans, but he admitted it nearly didn't happen. He said: 'It was down to what is recent and what's in the charts. I was originally going to do a mixture of "I Can Only Imagine" by David Guetta and Chris Brown and "This is Love" by will.i.am but it just didn't fit.

'"Starships" was massive at the time, and it just

worked really well and I loved playing it. Then I realised it fitted well with the Michael Jackson song, "Remember the Time", and that worked for the end.'

Of his summer tours, he said: 'It was crazy – V Festival was insane, performing there was a whole load of fun. I did a whole bunch of radio shows as well. I think the festivals are always a cool vibe because it's always a bit worrying because people choose to come to your stage and if your stage is empty, it's a bit like, "This isn't good", but luckily I absolutely rammed out the tent so I was really happy with that. So yeah, a lot of fun.'

With a hit record that cemented his standing as one of British music's brightest new talents, Conor now had the unenviable task of capitalising on his success. His sophomore effort would be 'Vegas Girl'. He said: 'It's more of a concept. The song has the lines, "shake like you're famous girl/like a Vegas Girl". Basically, it's this whole idea, like, a young party generation out having fun.'

It was one of the earliest songs recorded on the album, and came from Conor's desire to write a party song after watching a film about the fun times you have in Las Vegas, a city that is famous for its glitzy lights, gambling culture and a kitch and glamorous atmosphere.

He told *MaximumPop*: 'I came up with the tequila line. It was around halfway through the song and I thought it hadn't really shown off my vocals yet so I wanted to do something different and it just happened the tequila line was just before it, so we stuck with that.'

The video sees him colliding with a beautiful young girl outside a shop. After some awkward chat, he finally asks for her number. After he is politely turned down, the brazen pop star then asks if he can take a picture of her on his phone. She agrees, and in a nod to his rapid rise to stardom using social media, Conor subsequently uses his Twitter account to track down the girl – who just happens to be wearing a T-shirt emblazoned with the words 'Vegas Girl'.

He said: 'It was a weird thing to act and to try and make it normal. Also, until the day of the shoot we didn't know what we were going to be saying so it was a funny situation. It was odd, he [the director] was giving me weird ideas and I was saying, "No, I'm not doing that." So it was all about how I could get from meeting the girl in the video to taking her picture. There were some really dumb ideas.'

He told the *Guardian*: 'It's funny, because the director gave me four lines to get from bumping into her to taking her picture. We made up this scene where I asked if her shoulder was okay, told her I knew massage techniques, said I might need her number for insurance details. But they cut all of that out and just used the massage technique line, so I looked even more of a pervert!'

The director of 'Can't Say No' was in line to direct the second promo himself but he's glad that he didn't as his pitch inadvertently ended up being like Justin Bieber's 'Boyfriend' video. Rohan Blair-Mangat told this author: 'I was going to make his second video. I was pitching on it. They were like, "Write an idea and we'll go and make something." I guess I came up with several ideas. The idea that I settled with just wasn't working. I phoned up the commissioner and said I would still like to be involved with videos with him, but I don't think I was the right person for that time or I was bringing my strongest ideas, just because I thought it was a difficult song to make a video out of. He was talking about Vegas Girls and that kind of thing.

'And the idea I actually had, I'm glad I didn't make it. A few months after I pitched it, I saw the video for Justin Bieber's "Boyfriend". The idea for that video was the one I was going to make for Conor Maynard. Who knows when these videos are released, so Justin Bieber's would have been different or they would both come out at the same time and it would have looked strange, so I'm glad I didn't really push this idea.

'The things he talks about in "Vegas Girl" are captured pretty well in the video that they made. At the time the thing I was battling with was that you can't do anything in Vegas as he's not 21, and it also didn't feel right after the first video to go somewhere that isn't honest and authentic. So I was thinking where else could he be? I was thinking a car park in America somewhere, perhaps LA. There would be lots of cars and people partying. It's kind of about what do cool kids do – they can't go to bars, they can't go to casinos, so they make their own party and do their own thing. It would have been something different to the first video; it would have been a different party. It would have blazing sunshine and then it would have moved to the night, with car headlights shining on everyone and someone would have a speaker in the car, where the music was coming from. And that's really what Justin Bieber's video is. And I think that's exactly the same reason the director had. He would have been thinking, "Where am I going to set this?" and "What would Justin do?"

'I'm glad I didn't make that video because I don't

think it's fair to have those comparisons placed on him. They're completely different artists.' In the event the video was directed by Travis Kopach.

Conor added: 'The video was such a surreal situation. To have to walk up to a girl and ask for her number is just something I would never do. The conversation with the director, where we were choosing what to say, went on for ages; I thought it had to be realistic. The director suggested I said, "Oh, hey, you're really beautiful, can I have your number?" but I would never say that so we stuck with, "Hey, can I have your number? I know some good massage techniques!" and another line was, "Can I have your insurance number, because I think you've broken my heart!"'

While writing the song, he found it hard not to get excited about the possibility of shooting in Las Vegas and hitting the hot spots. 'Until I realised I am legally too young to go out in Vegas. So, the video would have consisted of me outside with the bouncers and me phoning my mum to pick me up – it wouldn't have been the best video,' Conor joked. 'So, the different idea behind it was you can be anywhere in the world, it didn't have to be Vegas, but you can still party like you're in Vegas. That's the idea behind the film.'

He later said of the girl in the New York shoot

at 5 Pointz in Queens when asked if they had a real-life romance: 'She was a really cool person to work with, on camera and off. I took her out as a thank you, I suppose, for everything she had done, a few days afterwards and she never called me back! No, I'm joking. I keep in contact with her and yeah, she's really cool.'

The song was once again written and produced by The Invisible Men, with additional production work from Parker & James. As previously, Conor also had a hand in penning the track, as did Dion Wardle and Scott Thomas.

Digital Spy wrote: '"I'll knock you down like you're Keri/ Forget your name like Rihanna," he insists over slick urban-light beats, with a voice that will undoubtedly draw comparisons to Justin Timberlake. The obvious clichés are all present and correct ("Roll the dice, I've got your number/ Hit the jackpot underneath the cover"), but he gets away with it, if only for his homage halfway through to "Tequila, Tequila, Tequila."'

However, the *Guardian* wasn't so impressed, writing: 'the 7pm, Asda mark-down value range version of Justin Bieber is back, with his own brand of lady-seducing. "I'll knock you down like Keri, forget your name like Rihanna," he sings. A great message for any teenage girl! And, er, set to almost exactly the same beat as his first single. The aggressive lyrics are weird, because Conor comes across as the kind of boy who'd do that "this must be your sister!" thing when he meets your mum, and ejaculate after 90 seconds of sex. Still, he's up for shots of tequila, and wants us to put our "head back/Lay it down like a Vegas girl", and that's hot. It's OK, he's 19! Everyone calm down.'

The *Gizzle Review* gave it just two out of five, observing: 'Like Bieber's latest effort, "Vegas Girl" is similarly full of references. I mean, the girl he's after is "looking so good with ya poker face", can "run the world [like] Queen B" and is "unthinkable" like Alicia. She's so hot he'll "forget your name like Rihanna". You don't stand a chance, Conor. No hard feelings. Otherwise this is déjà vu for Maynard compared with "Can't Say No". The beat is practically identical, with similarly grinding bass lines and swirling synths. It's certainly catchy, but it's unlikely to hit the same heights as his debut.

'And as for the boy who can't say no, spending his nights dreaming of women way out of his league, he just comes across as a horny teenager and a bit of a perv.'

It debuted on 21 July 2012 and it peaked at number four in the UK Singles Chart. For Conor, life was certainly changing, as he acknowledged to *FirstNews.co.uk*: 'It's been very hectic. I think it's been really unexpected, as I didn't know how it worked. You know, you release a song and maybe after a few weeks it starts to work its way up the charts and make the Top 20. But to get into the top two in its first week was pretty insane. I was obviously very thankful to the fans. It's been really fun. My average journey has changed quite a bit too. It now involves screaming, being chased, taking pictures, being followed and a lot of other things!'

Nine days later he would release his debut album, *Contrast*, and he had already revealed that he had high hopes, saying earlier: 'I didn't really want to come out with something that was really pop or cheesy, I really wanted to come out with something that was credible and I think I've got my way because the single is kind of a cool urban track. I am still recording for the album at the moment. In terms of songs that have actually been confirmed on the album there are probably around six or seven. I think the album will have a bit of something for everyone on there, really. It's going to be quite different from the covers I started with.'

He couldn't wait for the fans to hear his latest work, saying: 'I used to be excited just to upload a cover, and getting my mum into my room and showing her what I'd done. I'm just as excited about getting this album out – it's like that feeling again, but bigger.'

For his fans, the wait was finally over.

CHAPTER FIVE

A DEBUT TO REMEMBER

Conor told *The Edge*: 'Yeah, it took about two years for me to record my first album. So obviously the first year was just mainly trying to find the sound, find what kind of artist I was gonna be. We tried all kinds of different things and then as I kind of grew naturally as an artist and as a person, I just started to get more comfortable with who I wanted to be as an artist. I think the first song I ever recorded that made it on the album was "Vegas Girl". So we were like, "Yeah, this sounds kinda cool, let's keep going with this." I started recording.

'The Invisible Men were the main producers. When you're first signed, you start to learn whether you're an artist that wants to work with all the biggest producers in the world and then you make an album from that, or you try and build up a relationship with certain people and you find it through that way – I was more that way. I met The Invisible Men and worked with them, and I started to build up a relationship with them. They understood what I wanted as an artist and then we started working together loads, and the majority of the songs on my album were produced by them.'

When making the album, Conor had one motto and it would be the same one that he applied when he did his covers, reasoning it's better to fail in originality than to succeed in imitation. It's a mantra often repeated by him in interviews, but it's one he seems to genuinely believe in. He prides himself on the fact that his covers have had a different take on the original material, with a lot of them stripped down to just his melodic voice and a piano.

With his mission statement in hand, Conor set out to make an album that was far from the standard pop record. He had far loftier ambitions, telling AOL: 'I think I named my album *Contrast* because it's a contrast from what's already out there. I think that there are not really any albums or artists doing that exact thing. I want to be as successful as possible and I want as many people as possible listening to what I'm doing. So, I think if that happens, it will kind of, I suppose, change [pop music] in a way.'

It was a bold statement, but one borne of the kind of confidence that seems to have been instilled in Conor. It took two years for him to record the first album, with the first year trying to 'find the sound' and 'find what kind of artist I was gonna be'.

He told *Notion magazine*: 'After a year [of being signed], I really started to realise what sort of artist I wanted to be and what sound I wanted to move towards. It felt right. [I began to ask myself] "Am I the kind of artist who works with massive producers? How do I build a relationship with people?" Obviously I worked with some massive producers – a lot of the album was produced by The Invisible Men – and I realise for me that it's all about creating and building a relationship with those people so they can understand what I want. It's all about meeting people who can understand you as an artist.'

He added to *The Edge*: 'We tried all kinds of

different things and then as I kind of grew naturally as an artist and as a person, I just started to get more comfortable with who I wanted to be as an artist. I think the first song I ever recorded that made it on the album was "Vegas Girl". So we were like, "Yeah, this sounds kinda cool, let's keep going with this."'

When he began recording, it was the songwriting trio The Invisible Men who were the main producers. However, as a sign of just how much he and his team wanted the best for the album they made sure his record was packed with the latest stars. Given that his covers had not only brought him attention from music fans but also some of the biggest names in the industry, it made sense to call in some favours for album collaborations.

Connor added: 'As my sound got better and I got better, other big producers started getting involved and obviously I spent a week out in Miami with Pharrell Williams. I spent a week in New York and LA with Ne-Yo and Stargate. Frank Ocean wrote a song on my album as well, there's a track featuring Rita Ora. So yeah, I had a whole bunch of amazing experiences recording the album and I think a lot of it was just learning the writing process, being in the studio and just getting comfortable with it. There are so many things that go into being an artist now.'

While many felt that he had enjoyed a rapid rise to stardom, he had in fact been working on the album for a long period and had recorded around 200 songs – experimenting with different sounds and styles in a bid to discover what kind of recording artist he wanted to be. He said: 'I started in 2010 when I was 17. I'm 19 now so I've been working on my first album since then. It's taken a lot of turns and twists.'

Through all his experimenting, some things never changed. His direct influences on the album were Michael Jackson, Justin Timberlake, Usher and Drake. Of Drake, he said: 'One of the greatest inspirations to me right now has got to be Drake. I think he's an extremely talented artist and an extremely talented writer as well; I think the songs that he writes are so clever and really real, and you can really relate to it. He's definitely someone I'm really inspired by.'

In January 2013, he told MTV: 'I haven't met him yet. I might just have to get my stalker-mode on and just chase him down the street naked, begging to work with me! No, I'm joking!'

He added: 'I'm all about Drake at the moment. I went to his arena show at the O2 in London, and

it was a crazy experience. I went purely as a fan –
I didn't do the whole backstage thing. I knew
people that were going backstage, but I was like,
"No! I wanted the pure fan experience." I was
right at the back and at the top, but I did not care.
It was a bit crazy though, 'cos I ended up having
to take loads of pictures with random people who
recognised me. But yeah, he's a very inspiring
artist. His songs are really relatable.'

One of those songs was 'Marvin's Room', a
track full of self-loathing that features Drake
phoning his ex after a heavy drinking session. He
comes across as boastful over his perceived
superiority over her new lover and self-pitying as
he realises he is alone in the world. The loneliness
is complemented by the sparse bass beat and
muted keyboard sound.

The song was inspired by two encounters during
a session at the legendary Los Angeles Marvin's
Room studio. The first was an impromptu phone
call from music icon Stevie Wonder, asking if he
would like to meet up for a jam session.

Drake told *The LA Times*: 'He's one of the
kindest, most spontaneous individuals. He said,
"I'll be there in 20 minutes," so we started
cleaning up.

'I thought I was going to play the music and see

what he thought. But he goes in and starts playing the harmonica and starts adding all this production on this ballad, which I never even thought I'd do before. I'm like, "This is not happening."'

Ultimately, the session would end up being the song 'Take Care'. However, it's what happened after that became, arguably, Drake's biggest moment in music and also drove Conor to give his take on it to great acclaim from his fans. Inspired by Stevie Wonder's visit, Drake and producer Noah '40' Shebib continued to work, and soon the session would, thanks to a drunken phone call, end up with 'Marvin's Room'.

He continued: '[Shebib] started making this beat, and I started singing these melodies, and I got a phone call from this girl. I was in the booth, singing. I remember that was the first part I had.

'Middle of recording I got a call from this girl, and she had been drinking. Because I was recording, I just put the phone on the speaker and sat it on the music stand. "40" thought so quick to record it. I went back to recording more melodies. As I was recording, he was taking pieces of the conversation out – you know where the story is going. At the end of the night, we had a song called "Marvin's Room".

'Without Stevie being there, I don't know if I would have been as inspired to make that song. I wanted to make something that people did.'

Conor's cover proved to be a great favourite with the fans. Shot in black and white, and tight on his face, the video sees Conor at his most emotional. Face pained and lips close to the microphone, it's clear that this was a personal song, and one that his fans latched onto. With his voice at its most passionate, Conor was careful to ensure it wasn't drowned out by studio tricks on his debut album.

Previously, he has spoken out about the use of auto-tune technology: 'I think it's sometimes misunderstood as to what it is. Sometimes people think it allows you to be able to sing. Auto-tune doesn't do that – it's an effect on your voice. Some artists, like T-Pain and sometimes Chris Brown, turn it up to its fullest as a stylised effect, where you can really hear it, but with other artists you can't really hear it – there's just something there that makes things sound a bit more sweet. The difference between now and back then is it was all live instruments, and live instruments aren't perfect. Things could be slightly out of tune so singing slightly out of tune wouldn't get picked up. It all blended together and made the song, whereas now everything is so perfectly in tune through computers that if the voice was just a bit out of tune, it would stick out instantly. Auto-tune sweetens that, but obviously when you see an act play live you can see if they can sing or not for real. You can't use auto-tune live.

'While it has become a huge success, the early days of recording in the studio were less so.'

More accustomed to working in a bedroom with a webcam, Conor wasn't used to his new surroundings. The recording studio was packed with state-of-the-art equipment and whereas previously he could record cover songs in an intimate environment and work hard at it until he was satisfied, away from prying eyes, suddenly he was faced with producers, studio engineers and other musicians all watching him as he set about making his debut album.

He told the *Daily Star*: 'I've learned that music never goes according to plan. When I started making *Contrast*, I was awful because I'd never sung in a studio before. You could hear I was nervous, and it took some time to get comfortable singing in front of my producers.

'That's how *Contrast* came together in the first place. When I get into the studio again, I'll have to see what I'm feeling.'

It's not the first time that he suffered from stage fright, as he told the *Guardian*: 'I do always think back to my first concerts, where I was so nervous. I was in Brighton performing tracks from the album for the first time. I was so scared I didn't put on a good show; the audience focused on how nervous I was rather than the performance. I was literally gripping the microphone stand throughout the whole thing!'

Despite his fears, Conor was desperate to show off his singing and writing prowess. Not content with being blessed with a powerful voice he also wanted to show that he could also help write his own songs and not just sing videos. He told *IdolMag.co.uk*: 'I am trying to create as wide a variety as possible, though. With my covers I did "Only Girl In The World", through to a stripped-back piano cover of "Use Somebody" by Kings of Leon. I wanted to recreate that on my album. I've been working with some amazing names to accomplish that, so Pharrell, Ne-Yo, this is all on the first album so it was crazy for me.

'They had tracks ready and I wrote a lot while I was there. I also wrote a lot with Invisible Men, who co-wrote "Can't Say No" with me.'

He loved working with The Invisible Men. Despite their combined years in the industry, the songwriting trio were respectful of the young talent and took his opinions seriously. They could see that he was determined to have an impact on the songwriting and came to the studio armed with ideas.

Conor said in an interview to *Ink Splot*: 'At first people didn't really know I could write. I was my covers, so that didn't really mean I had to write anything. But when I was going to the studio, I'd definitely get involved in the writing. I'd learned from different writers, different producers, and my writing just slowly improved. And then, as it got closer to the album, I started writing more tracks with different producers, and the label would hear them, the management would hear them and be really impressed.'

In another interview he added: 'With The Invisible Men I'm the main writer, in that I sit down and figure out what I want to do with the song and they give their approval. Others like to work by themselves or have their own writing team.

'I'm still in the early stages of my career. I can't walk in and say, "This is how I'm going to do it" – I'm not one of those people who wants to do it their own way. I was lucky enough to be discovered [after] something I did by myself, but you have to sit back and learn from the people who have been in the industry longer than you.'

He continued to the BBC: 'There's a track on the album called "Just In Case", which I wrote with these producers. I don't know if I'm allowed to say it but another artist did try and take it – a very big American artist. And I was like, "Okay, it's mine." For me, that felt quite good, when someone you look up to tries to have it.'

Another contributor to the album was his old mentor, Ne-Yo. Conor told *Glamour* magazine: 'That started the whole kind of buzz, like, "Who's this kid Ne-Yo wants to sign?" Obviously, I ended up signing with EMI, because it was the best thing for me at the time. And there were no grudges down the line. Obviously, I've worked with Ne-Yo on this album, and he's featured on a lot of these tracks. And then Pharrell reached out to me to try and sign me, not realising that I'd already been signed and was about to start here in the UK. But he was like, "Well, I'd love to work with him anyway." So I flew out to America to work with him for the week. There are two tracks on the album that feature Pharrell.'

He enjoyed working with Pharrell Williams, describing him as a 'humble, cool man' during their time together in the studio. When not making music, the pair would spend hours playing Mario Kart on the Wii.

Of their track 'Lift Off', he said: 'We took a chance with that. It doesn't sound like anything else out right now so I had no idea how it would fit in. I'm so happy we went with it – it's become one of my favourites.' They also worked together on 'Glass Girl' – a soulful track that saw his fans compare him, once again, to Justin Timberlake.

Of the superstar collaboration he said: 'It was crazy. I got to meet a lot of people – I met more people in that week than I've met in my entire life. Obviously, Pharrell was there, and then on the third day Ludacris just rolled into the studio to listen to the music. And Tyler, The Creator rolled in as well. And then right at the end, on the last day, Pharrell took us to this Tyler, The Creator concert in Miami, and I just remember I was standing with Pharrell on my right shoulder and Lil Wayne on my left, just chillin'. It was pretty cool, they're pretty cool guys.'

Conor described his first meeting with Pharrell Williams to *ilikemusic.com*: 'It started when I'd just finished my showcase for the record label, a few weeks before my first show in London. The head of the label was there, and he came up to me afterwards with the vice-president and told me that he loved it. Then they looked at each other and were like, "Shall we tell him?" I was like, "What? Tell me!" I got really excited, and then they told me, "Pharrell has been on the phone, and he would love to work with you." I couldn't believe it. I literally felt like I was going to wet myself! I was like, [really high-pitched] "Oh my god!"'

He went to Miami for a week to meet Pharrell while working on his album, but worried that when he got there the legendary producer might not remember him. However, a relieved Conor explained: 'Actually, when I got there he might have been more excited to meet me than I was to meet him! It was crazy. He was really ready to go, had all these ideas and he told me he'd actually been watching me for about three years, watching my progress.

'The funny thing is, when he actually reached out to work with me it was to sign me. He didn't realise I was signed – he thought I was just doing YouTube covers. He was like, "Damn, I missed my chance! You know what, I'm going to work with him anyway." I went out there for a week, and I must have met more famous people in that week than I have in my entire life.

He added to the BBC: 'I don't know why. I

didn't know much about it. His people got in touch with the label that I'm signed to and said we want to work with your kid. I was like, wow, how does he even know who I am? This is crazy – this is even before *Contrast* was even released. This was when I was still recording the album. I was really worried about it but I met him, and he was literally more excited about meeting me than I was [him] – how do you know who I am? I met his partner and their child. And when she was pregnant with him, she showed Pharrell my covers. I think it was a Justin Timberlake, which he produced and wrote. He kind of saw it and was really impressed. Apparently, he had been following my covers for two years before he made the call. And the reason he made the call was because he heard about the MTV brand new thing. He wanted to sign me to his own label, but then he found out I had already been signed, so he said he would love to work with me anyway. It was such a crazy week – Monday to Friday.'

He added: 'When I flew out to Miami for a week to work on the album and find some tracks, Ne-Yo's people found out I was out there. I had to extend my stay, which was annoying as I had only packed for a week.'

Conor then said about another track called

'Drowning': 'Even though that one wasn't written by me, I really understood it because I've been through break-ups myself – I put my own twist on it.'

In another interview, he added to *The Edge*: 'Yeah, "Animal" is definitely one of my favourites! "Animal" is the first song on the album and then another one of my favourites is "Just in Case", which is at the end of the album – I like that one as well. "Turn Around" is one of my favourites as well. But it's cool because "Animal" and "Just in Case", I actually wrote them as well.'

While making the album, he kept his fans updated, tweeting to say: 'Last day in the studio in LA! Then tomorrow got the 12-hour flight home...someone hold me.'

Previously he had tweeted: 'Mad time in Miami so far!! Might have to extend this trip you know... #only gettingbetter,' – before posting a picture of himself with the Neptunes star: 'Just casually being cool dudes in the studio...kinda.'

And the superstar collaborations weren't finished there either. Another collaborator was new soul superstar Frank Ocean. Conor told *The Arts Desk*: 'That was crazy for me. His producers were over in London and they'd seen my covers on YouTube and got in touch with people who worked with me. I met them in a studio and they played me a few songs, some written by Frank, some not. Then I heard "Pictures" and thought, "I love that song", and Frank Ocean was singing the demo so that was the one I wanted to record. Annoyingly I never got to meet him but hopefully in the future I will. I feel like he's a rare artist that's allowed RnB to live in the now, like a lot of artists have stopped doing that, but he's really continued it.'

The producers were Midi Mafia – a music production duo comprising of Bruce Waynne and Dirty Swift.

Swift said: 'We just did a bunch of stuff in the UK for this artist named Conor Maynard. He won MTV's Brand New For 2012. He's getting a lot of support over there.'

Bruce Waynne told BBC Radio 1: 'You know when he came in the room, he was unassuming. When we meet someone, especially like Conor, we go, "Okay, he's signed, does the label believe in him, are they supporting him?" Then the next thing we look at is what's his work ethic? Is this person going to represent what we're doing to the best of his abilities? And when we met him that's how we felt. I had this record that Frank Ocean wrote and I thought it just felt right.'

Of the track, Conor said: 'Yeah, it is quite racy in places. The lyrical content is crazy. Frank always writes some mad lyrics but it adds to the vibe, it adds to the flavour. I wanted an album that took people by surprise, musically and lyrically. I didn't want everyone to catch everything the first time round.'

Conor talked to MTV about Frank Ocean: 'He's blowing up right now. For me, it's crazy to watch that he's a proper, true kind of R&B singer, and he's still kind of out there doing really well.

'It's sometimes difficult for RnB singers to make people want to listen. It's one of those genres that almost faded to the background a little bit and it's people trying to bring it back, and he's doing an amazing job of that.

'I never got to meet him. It was one of those sessions where a song is put out there, where someone writes it, and someone else hears it and I end up with a song on my album. For me, it's kind of annoying I never got to meet him, but at the same time it's an incredible song.'

He added: '"Pictures" is one of my favourite songs on the album.

'I never got to meet him but yes, he wrote the song, the guys that produced it met me in the UK. They're called Midi Mafia – they loved my sound and said, "We've got this song that Frank Ocean wrote, we'd love you to have it! We'd love you to record it!" I heard it and I loved it, so that was cool.'

Frank Ocean is one of soul music's new stars, but he caused a stir after he talked openly about his sexuality in the summer of 2012. Originally expected to debut as sleeve notes for the then new album *Channel Orange*, he instead posted a message on his Tumblr page.

He wrote: '4 summers ago, I met somebody. I was 19 years old. He was too. We spent that summer, and the summer after, together. Every day almost. And on the days we were together, time would glide. Most of the day I'd see him, and his smile.

'Sleep I would often share with him. By the time I realised I was in love, it was malignant. It was hopeless. There was no escaping; no negotiating to the women I had been with, the ones I cared for and thought I was in love with. I sat there and told my friend how I felt. I wept as the words left my mouth. I grieved for then. Knowing I could never take them back for myself. He patted my back. He said kind things. He did his best, but he wouldn't admit the same. He had to go back inside soon. It was late and his girlfriend was waiting for him upstairs. He wouldn't tell the truth about his feelings for me for another three years. I felt like I'd only imagined reciprocity for years.'

The singer decided to release the letter after a journalist 'very harmlessly' wrote that he often used male pronouns in songs.

Telling *GQ*, Ocean said: 'I was just like, "Fuck it! Talk about it, don't talk about it. No more mystery. Through with that." The night I posted it, I cried like a fucking baby.' He continued: 'It was like all the frequency just clicked to a change in my head. All the receptors were now receiving a different signal, and I was happy. I hadn't been happy in so long. I've been sad again since, but it's a totally different take on sad. There's just some magic in truth and honesty and openness.'

Conor spoke out in support of the RnB star, telling *Glamour* magazine: 'For me, it was a shock. Like, no one expected it coming. But I think it's great. It's amazing that we're in a place in time now where people can do that, and it's obviously a big thing to do, and it must have been really scary to think what people were going to think. For me, it was extremely brave to do that and I really respect that he has already built up this big following and no one knows, or had any idea. I've seen all the respect he's been getting on Twitter, it's really cool to see that. It would be awful to think that people would think badly of it. And also, the song he's written for the album is incredible, regardless of whether he's gay or not. I'm happy to have that, and happy to have him on the album.'

Conor went on to reveal what the song was about, saying: 'He's saying he was with someone, and while he was with them he used to take a lot of pictures, like a lot of couples do – on Facebook. Anyway, they broke up and the person took those pictures away and burnt them or whatever. So he could never look at them to remember exactly how it happened. It's a situation where you have broken up and you just want to look back at it but you can't. It's a horrible feeling.'

And in an interview with BBC Radio 1's Nick Grimshaw, he added: 'I loved this. I loved the song and I wanted a track written by Frank Ocean. It was such an honour and I really look up to him. He brought RnB into the modern world.'

Another collaborator is Rita Ora. Born in Kosovo but raised in London, the RnB singer landed her big break after she was spotted by one of Jay-Z's team following an open mic performance. She subsequently landed a deal with Roc Nation – Jay-Z's record label. A single 'Hot Right Now' with DJ Fresh topped the UK charts in early 2012.

Conor and Rita Ora shared the same manager

and the two stars first met while babysitting the manager's twins. Conor recalled: 'I actually met her before we got to work with each other. We are both kind of under the same management so I've known her for quite a while. I remember when she used to play me her stuff, and now it's just blown up for both of us at the same time. I'm just really happy we got to go into the studio before all that happened because right now it'd be absolutely crazy trying to get a duet with her.'

It would turn out to be an eventful babysitting gig, with one of the twins throwing up on Rita.

Conor said: 'Rita's crazy. She's actually an old friend of mine, so I knew her from before. When we got in the studio together, it really worked well. When you hear the track, it's a track that fits what we're about. We couldn't have sung a love song together, because everyone would know that it wouldn't be real so I think for us, it was a clever thing we came up with.'

He added to the BBC: 'She's so much fun. It's really weird because she has these pockets of genius. We were writing our parts with a writer in the room – all just vibing off each other. She started coming up with these lines, just singing them. And we were like, write them down – she would have these random outbursts.'

Rita told *Teen Vogue*: 'The moment I met Conor Maynard in London two years ago, we had an instant connection; I knew we had to work together. There's something special about him and that voice! He was discovered on YouTube at age 17 by the one and only Ne-Yo (Conor's cover of "Beautiful Monster" caught his eye), and his recent debut album, *Contrast*, is going to be huge (it already is in the U.K.!). I call his musical style "urban pop". His second U.S. single, "Turn Around" (featuring Ne-Yo), is awesome, but be sure to check out "Lift Off" (written and produced by Pharrell) and our song, "Better Than You", which we wrote after having sing-offs in our spare time. While Conor's voice has opened doors, his personality will take him even further: He's a humble, down-to-earth jokester. And the girls love him! The future will bring nothing but hits and success for Conor, and I'm looking forward to following his journey.'

Conor talked about the last song on the album 'Just In Case' to *FirstNews.co.uk*: 'That's the last track on the album, funnily enough, and that's at the opposite end of the spectrum. It's very chilled. It's about a previous relationship that I was in that I wrote this song about, that I'd gone through before.

'When we were in the studio we took forever to finish the song because we were just hanging out. It wasn't like work! I think those sessions are the best.'

He told *Teen Vogue*: 'I like to mess around and have fun. I don't take things too seriously. There's a track featuring Rita on my album, and when we recorded it, it was literally one of the funniest days. We just messed around and somehow came out with a song at the end of the day. I never like to focus too hard in terms of sitting and writing; I'd rather just come up with ideas, run with it, and have fun.'

Conor couldn't believe his luck to work with the artists he worked with at such a tender age, stating matter-of-factly to *KidzWorld*: 'It was crazy working with them on my first album. Obviously, it was a dream of mine to work with such prominent artists/producers in the music industry but I thought that would happen on perhaps the 2nd/3rd album, not before I've even released a first single! They both found out about me through my YouTube covers, and watched my progress before they reached out, both initially trying to sign me! Which was even MORE crazy! But yeah, working with them was just incredible as I saw creativity on the next level. They are amazing at what they do, and I think it will be a while before I meet anyone else that compares.'

With a steely determination, he added: 'For the album I do want to recreate the quality I gave when recording those covers for YouTube, but in a different way because it's been around two years since I recorded them so I have grown as a person as well as an artist since then – my head isn't in the same space now as it was back when I originally recorded those covers. I have a different taste in music, I also listen to a lot of Drake so that kind of influenced me to come out with this urban kind of sound.'

'Turn Around', which was written by Ne-Yo, was recorded quickly in a Los Angeles recording studio.

Conor said: 'It's one of the last ones we did for the album and it wasn't a song we ever expected to happen. [Producers] Stargate heard I was working with Ne-Yo and sent it over there and then. It really ties the album together; I'm so glad we happened to get it in time.'

Of the song 'Mary Go Round' he said: 'I wrote that about a relationship I'd been in. And for "Animal", I wanted a song that I'd dance to in a club with my friends, but wasn't your typical Euro-Dance track. That's not cool to me – I had no interest in going down that route.'

On the album sleeve notes he gave a special mention to EMI A&R Elias Christidis and Parlophone president Miles Leonard. He later explained: 'They were the ones who believed in me from the start. They really took a step forward and were the people who brought me in. I got along with them the best and they were really positive and confident about me as an artist. They've become friends.'

He said of the reviews on the album: 'I remember my first ever album review and the first thing they said was, "Oh yeah, we were really expecting a very Justin Bieber kind of pop-y album, and it really wasn't that," and I was like, "Well, I tried to tell you."'

He added: 'When you go to events and stuff, maybe like shows, I suppose you've got to think about it. Sometimes you worry about being an artist or a celebrity. You don't want to walk out and a random tabloid pick some random thing. You see it happen to other people and it's not nice. You sometimes feel a bit self-conscious about that. I'm a 19-year-old guy but I think if I was a girl or something like that, it would be worse. Luckily I get the less worse end of it. They're being kind to me at the moment – I ignore it.'

Confident that he had the songs down and the

superstar collaborations in place, all that was left was the cover. Conor explained: 'There were two photo shoots done for it, one in London and one in America. We had this photo shoot in London way before album was released and actually went with a picture from that shoot as the cover. Photo shoots are a chance to experiment with looks and ideas. I try and play music I enjoy for a photo shoot to get me in the vibe of having fun in front of the camera, not feeling weird, just doing it. The person pulling my tie, that's actually a woman named Julia. That photo shoot was taken while I was doing the "Vegas Girl" video shoot in New York and she was my behind-the-scenes camera girl. She's still a close friend now so that's really cool. She had a very good grip on my tie – good hands.'

The *Guardian* said of the album: 'Maynard's album is much more sonically sophisticated, and far slicker, than a record by a teen-market singer has any right to be. His insanely catchy number two hit from last April, "Can't Say No", might be all about how much he likes girls – a theme that's the bread, butter, alpha and omega of teen pop – but its snaking bass line and minimal R&B beats penetrate far deeper into the zone of gnarly club R&B than One Direction would ever dare. "Vegas

Girl", its successor, is just as bass-heavy, full of whispered urban urgency and graced by a little show-offy a cappella line about tequila. If we are to have ersatz urban pop-lite, it can definitely sound like this.'

Digital Spy observed: 'You can't blame Conor Maynard's frustration over constantly being compared to Justin Bieber. The Canadian teen has made it impossible to transcend from YouTube sensation to fully-fledged pop star without drawing comparisons, particularly when Maynard is one of the web's biggest success stories in recent memory. While Conor's lady-killer swag may not come across wholly convincing, his debut set remains an enjoyable introduction that will help shake off those more pesky comparisons.'

And the BBC raved: 'Girls love him, even though he can't need to shave more than twice a week. And he got his break by posting cover versions on YouTube. But still, British pop upstart Conor Maynard really hates being compared to Justin Bieber. Listening to his debut album, it's clear Maynard has a point. This is a credible collection of electronic RnB tracks that owes a greater debt to another, more grown up Justin, the one pop lost to Hollywood. It's derivative, but in the best possible way; Maynard's songs do a good job of incorporating current dance and urban trends into some very catchy pop tunes...

'The artists Maynard used to cover from his Brighton bedroom remain an influence on him: *Contrast* has moments that recall Chris Brown, Ne-Yo and Usher while his producers are particularly fond of the dancehall drum sounds used on recent Rihanna hits. But it's clearly Timberlake who's the touchstone; his presence is felt every time Maynard breaks into falsetto. Meanwhile, a song called "Glass Girl" is essentially an attempt to rewrite JT's "Cry Me a River" for the dub step generation. Like most of the album, it works.'

Contact Music said: 'What's important to note is that with music such as this, which is aimed so clearly, so directly and with such force at the hormonal teen market, you're not evaluating artistry, you are evaluating science. The science of pop. The exact formula of successful pop music mutates and evolves over time but it almost always includes a cocktail of haircuts, vocoders, expensive trainers, auto-tune facilities, big choruses, the influence of former successful pop artists, lucrative guest vocalists, synthetic drum beats and manufactured sex appeal (of the kind that is specifically designed to make you question your own morality/sexuality/psychological wellbeing, should you fall under its spell).'

However, they also noted that some elements of the production were a little unbalanced. In particular, they felt that Ne-Yo and Pharrell's guest vocals detracted from Maynard's power. They said: 'It's only when he's paired up with Rita Ora that the combination works, as the bleach-blonde vamp well and truly puts Maynard in his place on "Better Than You". The chemistry of their voices is one of the more appealing aspects of the album. You can hear the cash registers ringing on that one.'

A lot of critics noted that the lyrical content featured several references to partying and women. Not that Conor apologises for this.

He told *Glamour* magazine: 'I think it relates to most 19-year-old boys' lifestyles. I think being 19 and being a guy, a lot of my time, other than doing music, is about partying with mates and girls. Those are the two main aspects of my life. I don't think I've got anything else to focus on right now, apart from eating. And I'm not going to write an album about food. So those are the two main things I like to write about.'

He announced his album on Twitter tweeting: 'Firstly, my debut album, titled "Contrast" is now available to Pre-Order on iTunes here!! So go go RT RT!! #Contrast.'

As the day of the album's release grew closer and closer on 30 June, Conor began to get nervous, filled with apprehension as to what position his debut album would chart. 'That's the scary part, the one nerve-wracking bit, but we'll have to see what happens,' he admitted to *Entertainment Wise*.

And when asked what he would do if it did make it number one, he said: 'I'd probably go back to Brighton and have some mad, mad party with all my friends and probably wake up regretting it all the next morning!'

While the album only sold 17,000 copies, it debuted at number one in the UK.

Conor said: 'It was kind of a really, really horrible week. You got told every day where it is in the charts, and you can kind of tell – but it was so close. And then you have three whole days of not knowing where you're going to be until the actual day when it is announced. When I was told it's number one, I was like, "Oh, my goodness".'

However, while delighted with the success, he was disappointed when, on a night out to celebrate his album win, the baby-faced star was asked for ID at London hotspot, Whisky Mist.

He said of his success to *FemaleFirst*: 'It was

incredible, that was probably the highlight of my career so far. Obviously everything, working with those people, travelling around the world, it all went into that. It was definitely the highlight so far.'

He added: 'Absolutely amazing! It doesn't even feel real at the moment. That was my only main aim – to get my album to number one – and for it to have done it, so quickly too, is definitely a highlight for me. It's crazy!'

A criticism from his early fans was that the album had little of what made them love him so much. A passionate rendition of 'Use Somebody' by Kings of Leon, which saw a young Conor close his eyes tightly as he sang, still attracts scores of comments on YouTube, asking for him to sing songs like that rather than his high temp fare.

In August 2011 he posted a rendition of 'Back To Black' and 'Valerie' – 'Yoooooo everyone!!! Thank you for taking part in the Facebook poll here's what you asked for!!! maybe with a little twist :) hahaaa, But yeah here's my farewell to an absolutely amazing artist, who will not be forgotten any time soon. R.I.P. Amy Winehouse.'

One comment read: 'The annoying thing is, Conor has the voice for this type of music but his producers think, "Oh EVERYONE loves pop, let's make him a idiot singing about girls and money."'

Conor talked about the lack of ballads to the *Sun*: 'When I was singing covers I did a lot of ballads, so I thought with this album I'd go in a new direction.

'The track "Pictures" is sort of a modern-day ballad. It's written by Frank Ocean, who is incredibly talented.'

But he refused to rest on his laurels, saying: 'I am funny when it comes to that kind of thing, when it comes to thinking I've made it: there is always another milestone, another goal to achieve. When my album was number one in the UK, everyone was going crazy. Every time I reach a new goal, I want to go to the next level. Even if I have an album that goes number one worldwide I would be like, now I want two albums to go to number one worldwide. It is always about reaching that next goal. For me, I don't know when I will be able to say I have made it, I have done it. It is going to take something pretty big to do that.'

Conor's next single would be 'Turn Around' featuring his mentor, Ne-Yo. The high-octane song vindicated the hype attributed to Ne-Yo's protégé. It was a catchy track designed to get you on the dance floor, with the video showcasing a more mature Conor. Sharing space with his mentor on the dance floor, or in this case, a city street in the dead of the night and a black-out studio, seemed to have brought out the best in Conor, strutting, posing and putting on a performance that equalled Ne-Yo's. It was an accomplished video that saw the hooded singer pull off some moves on the city street, as well as getting up and close with a young actress in a suspended phone booth.

The action-packed shoot also saw Conor and the beauty surf on a moving bus, a stunt described by Conor as 'The Kill Conor concept'. Directed by Colin Tilley, the video was set in Los Angeles and a behind-the-scenes shoot saw Ne-Yo and Conor larking about on set, with Conor jokingly chiding the pop superstar for doing too much in *his* video: 'It's meant to be only featuring Ne-Yo' – as Ne-Yo had a laugh trying to do everything he could to upstage him by dancing in front of him and shoving his hat in his face. Director Tilley declared that Conor, as usual, 'killed it'. Ne-Yo spiced it out: 'We're feeling really good about the video.'

Conor said of the video to *FemaleFirst*: 'That would be the director. He had his ideas, and that was one of them. I literally had to get in a phone booth and hang 80 feet in the air on a crane. That wasn't fake – it was all real. You can see on the behind-the-scenes me in the phone booth. It was mental; it was a really fun video shoot.

Of working with Ne-Yo, Conor said to *Student Pocket Guide*: 'It's crazy. For me, the first time I got to meet him was an insane moment. He was someone that I used to listen to growing up and then suddenly I was in a room with him, talking to me about music. It was crazy, and obviously to get the chance to work with him just blew that first moment out of the water! I did the single with him, the music video with him, performed with him, all of that stuff. He's become a mentor, not only musically but as a person as well. He's had all these hits but he's so cool and down to earth.'

Conor said at the time: 'I don't think I'm going to shoot a video better than this.'

Ne-Yo chided: 'He won't, until we work together again.'

Conor said about the song: 'It's one of the last ones we did for the album and it wasn't a song we ever expected to happen. Stargate heard I was working with Ne-Yo and sent it over there and then. It really ties the album together – I'm so glad we happened to get it in time.'

It peaked at number eight in the UK charts, further cementing his pop star status and showcasing a more mature sound.

Yahoo wrote: 'It could be argued that Conor Maynard is the UK's answer to Justin Bieber. Though not enjoying quite the same success as the Biebs, the two young musicians' stories bear some striking similarities.

'Much like Mr Bieber, Conor came to the attention of a US mega star after sharing videos of himself singing a number of covers on YouTube. After seeing Conor's cover of his own hit, "Beautiful Monster", Ne-Yo got in contact with the then 16-year-old, becoming and since remaining his mentor.

'Following the success of "Can't Say No", "Vegas Girl" and number one début album *Contrast*, Conor returns with another assault on the chart, joined by aforementioned mentor, Ne-Yo. Where Justin Bieber pandered to his younger fan base with songs like "Baby" and "Somebody To Love" in the early stages of his career, Conor Maynard has skipped ahead to making music that his generation would listen to. Ne-Yo and Conor's vocals are surprisingly well matched on the song, begging the question, why wasn't the single released sooner? While his first two singles were catchy enough, "Turn Around" is by far Conor's strongest single to date. The bass thumping club track is a step in the right direction for Conor and with Ne-Yo by his side, who knows, maybe one day he will surpass the mighty Bieber.'

Digital Spy raved: 'Poor Conor Maynard may have been cruelly dumped by his girlfriend over MSN Messenger when he was 13, but it's safe to say things have picked up tenfold since. However, despite now being a fully-fledged chart-topping act, don't expect him to start being the meanie who does the dumping. "Turn around, open your eyes/Look at me now/Turn around, girl I've got you/We won't fall down," he promises his (hopefully more appreciative) new beau over a mix of euphoric Italo piano riffs and pacing house beats, all worthy of the air-grabbing displayed in the accompanying music video. With mentor and pal Ne-Yo joining him on the track and another pop hit to add to his blossoming collection, we're sure being ditched over the internet will safely remain in Conor's past.'

NME was less enthusiastic, however, writing: 'Brighton's fledgling heart-throb Conor Maynard emotes intense, slightly nonsensical lyrics like, "Uh baby, we're so high now, whoa/'Til our worries end our pain right now". Christ man, you're hardly out of short trousers – chill the fuck out or I envisage dysfunction in adulthood. Meanwhile, Ne-Yo plays the Fonzy role (thinks he's cool, hangs out with kids), phones it in and saves the writing team the job of coming up with a middle-eight.' The majority of critics, however, were more taken with his debut effort, noting that this was not a social networking phenomenon with a novelty sell-by date. While he made his name singing covers on YouTube, it was clear from his debut album, filled with songs that he helped create, that Conor Maynard was the real thing.

CHAPTER SIX

CONOR MAYNIA TAKES HOLD

A common theme surrounding Conor Maynard is that of someone who hasn't been changed by fame. Of course, superstardom is a new thing for him but there are signs that he will never forget his roots. Friends who have known him for years claim he is still the same person. This author has spoken to several such friends. And while they didn't want to go on record about their time with the young superstar, all, without fail, couldn't resist mentioning that fame hasn't changed him.

During an interview for this book, Anth Melo claimed: 'He's definitely the same Conor that you see in interviews and on TV. He's hilarious, always making jokes. He could literally take the awkwardness out of any situation just by being himself. He's humble, he's down to earth – always a great guy to have around. Always somebody you can count on. He always remembers his roots and how he got to where he is today. I'm so proud of Conor and everything he has accomplished. He really does deserve it all. He worked his ass off to get where he is today. I know more than anybody how much work he truly had to put in this, so it's amazing to see it all finally happen for him. All of this is only the beginning; all of this is nothing compared to how big and successful Conor will be in the future. He's destined for the best and the greatest.'

Conor himself said to *FlavourMag*: 'I always kept my closest friends as the ones that were there, I know exactly who they are. I mean, there have been changes, people who hit me up non-stop and it's a bit like, you never used to do this before all this. I just kind of shrug it off – you weren't really my close friend before and I don't think you are now.' But he didn't need to worry about making new friends for too long. With his stock rising, it wasn't long before he was becoming pally with the world's biggest superstars.

One particular encounter saw him flying high. Pop superstar Rihanna approached him during a flight from Los Angeles to London.

After his chair was tapped, the Brighton boy was lost for words when he turned around to see the dance pop and RnB beauty. He told the *Sun*: 'I just stared at her. She said, "Hi. Congratulations on everything!" and then she wandered off.

'I tried to say something but I just kind of went, "Er, um, er", and that's all that came out. It really wasn't that great as a reply. I just couldn't believe it. That's the most starstruck I have ever been.'

He added: 'Getting to work with Pharrell [Williams] was exciting but I had 17 hours a day to get prepared to meet him, but this, it was just unexpected.'

Conor also became pals with Olympic star Tom Daley after they struck up a Twitter friendship. He told the *Daily Star*: 'I've been chatting to Tom and I didn't realise but he's a big fan. He said he'd love to come along to a gig some time, so we are trying to arrange.'

Maynard also took time to blast the Twitter troll who became a national hate figure after he attacked Daley, following his synchronised diving performance at the London Olympics in the summer of 2012.

'It's not fair when people overstep the mark because they are invisible on a computer,' he said. 'It's just cowardly to attack someone over the internet, but in Tom's case karma came and smacked that kid round the face.

'The best bit for me was seeing the backlash that kid got and the amount of support there is for our athletes.'

Daley retweeted the offensive message, which read: 'You let your dad down I hope you know that.'

The 18-year-old, whose father Robert had died of a brain tumour in 2011, received huge support from the social media world following the hateful tweet.

The Twitter user had also commented: 'Hope your crying now you should be why can't you even produce for your country your just a diver anyway a over-hyped prick. You really didn't try your best Tommy you said you'd do your country proud and you let us all down rather support a tramp tbh.'

Later, the same user apologised, saying: 'I'm sorry mate I just wanted you to win cause it's the Olympics I'm just annoyed Tom accept my apology.'

But his contrition seemed to be short-lived, as he sent out a further series of vile tweets: 'Why don't you respond to me you pr*ck stop getting me hate alright I've said I'm sorry now fuck off,' and 'Where are you now you little p***y?'

He went on to write: 'I'm going to find you and I'm going to drown you in the pool you cocky tw*t you're a nobody people like you make me sick.'

The Twitter user had made his comments after Tom Daley and diving partner, Peter Waterfield, finished in fourth place. Daley said at the time: 'Gutted so sorry everyone but we tried our best and you can't afford to miss a dive at this standard bring on individual!'

And he certainly did bring it on, winning Bronze in the men's 10m platform. Conor was quick to praise the 18-year-old on Twitter. He wrote: 'Can't watch the diving cuz I'm stuck in some airport but seeing a running commentary on my timeline! :) YES @TomDaley1994 !!! #DidUsProud'.

The pair have since been spotted enjoying nights out together at several London hotspots. Conor told the *Telegraph*: 'I'm really enjoying partying at the moment. I'd spoken to Tom Daley on Twitter before, but I met him in a club recently and we were hanging out with Liam from One Direction. When a fan spotted us, her head almost exploded, she was so excited. I love all the attention because it means my music is getting out there – that's all I've ever wanted.'

During the summer of 2012, Conor was certainly caught up in Olympic fever. He appeared on stage at London's G.A.Y., backed by female dancers wearing Team GB swimsuits. However, while everything he touched seemed to turn to gold at that moment, he found himself in the firing line after his inclusion as one of the performances at the 2012 Mobo Awards saw him being criticised by Labrinth. The singer was so bemused at seeing Conor and Ed Sheeran at the show that he believed the ceremony should change its name. Labrinth told the *Daily Star*: 'I think it is a bit weird because Ed Sheeran doesn't make black music, and neither does Conor Maynard – he makes commercial pop.

'Even I'm not making black music. It's commercial music, but at least it is more related to hip-hop so it makes more sense. I don't think it should be called the Music Of Black Origin anymore. It should be Music Of Urban Origin, or just Music Awards.'

Conor hit back, telling the BBC: 'I grew up listening to people like Michael Jackson and Stevie Wonder, and a lot of my musical influences are black artists.'

JLS star Jonathan 'JB' Gill also said: 'I don't think that Music of Black Origin is any longer unrepresented.

'A few years ago guys like Wiley and Dizzee Rascal might not have been recognised, now they're getting to number one. That's an incredible step for Music of Black Origin and the Mobo Awards. They're definitely starting to put a lot of artists on the map.'

Mobo founder Kanya King added: 'The gospel winner, the jazz winner – where else are they going to get a platform? Who else is going to champion them?

'And it's amazing to have someone like Dionne Warwick on the same stage as some of the up-and-coming stars. It helps to bring it to a global audience. Our work is never done.'

Warwick, celebrated for hits such as 'Heartbreaker' and 'Walk On By', said that without black music, 'you wouldn't have any music.' But when asked what she thought of the current crop of artists she had seen performing at the ceremony, she replied: 'It's been, er, interesting.'

Despite the criticisms, Conor was still happy being at the ceremony, telling the *Liverpool Echo*: 'I'm having a great time. I can't wait for the MOBOs. I came to Liverpool this summer. I played at the O2 Academy and we had a fantastic night. The crowd were so loud, so into it. It was one of those dates that really stands out on a tour.

MOBO is like that, too – a really appreciative audience. So when they put those two elements together – whoa, it's going to be awesome.'

In August 2012, he announced his full UK tour. From 24 October he played several big gigs across Great Britain, comprising Brighton Dome, Norwich UEA, Leicester O2 Academy, Bristol Academy, London O2 Shepherds Bush Empire, Leeds Metropolitan University, Bournemouth O2 Academy, Glasgow O2 ABC, Newcastle O2 Academy, Manchester HMV Ritz and Birmingham HMV Institute.

He said: 'I think it will be really fun; this is my first tour where the fans have actually had the album. It's been out already, they've had a chance to listen to it – you know listen to the album to find out which songs they like. They've had that side of the listening experience and I think it's time to give them another experience of listening to my music and trying to make it more interactive. I look at it when I'm doing a show not me performing to them but more me partying with them.'

Anth Melo supported him on tour, and he was delighted to be working again with his old pal. In an interview for this book, he said: 'Joining Conor on tour was crazy. It was probably one of my favourite times I've had in my life so far. Touring together was something we've always talked about from the very beginning. Seeing it finally happen and actually becoming a reality was insane. It was awesome getting to finally meet fans that I've never met before, some dating back from the first "OMG" cover. It was just incredible being able to share the stage every single night together; we had a lot of fun, on stage and off stage. We definitely made the best of that tour.'

One of those shows was a sell-out in London. Melo observed: 'That was insane! It was one of my first shows in London – I had an amazing time. It was a nerve-wracking thing to look forward to, just because it was my first time performing my original material in front of fans. They'd been waiting so long to hear it, and I'd been waiting so long to show it to them: it was a big moment. Now I'm just looking forward to doing the next one and the next one.'

He had been rehearsing vigorously and tweeted: 'Start rehearsals for tour soon...anything you guys wanna see? :) no nip slips. Day 2 of rehearsals. one word sweating. I must just rehearse naked.'

And he told *Hits Radio*: 'It's not like you suddenly get up there and it's amazing, you need to do rehearsals. I have a choreographer, but not for dancing – it's more for movement on stage – when do I run to the left, when do I run to the right? I started to notice that with my songs I was starting to do the same thing – I just run around. And sometimes I need to be a bit more structured. I wanted to work with someone who can help me with the structure. You find the songs that need a lot of running around and jumping around but some songs just need your feet planted on the ground. You've just got to figure it out – it's all about vocal acting. I actually got really good advice. It's a bit of a name drop here: I was speaking to Jessie J about performing and we were both talking about vocal acting. It's all about really believing what you're singing and showing that to the audience. It helps.'

He added: 'I didn't even know what to say at some points, and I just stood there to take it all in. It was so cool to see the Conor Maynard poster and then "sold out" next to it – that felt good.'

What also felt good was being bombarded by skimpy underwear at the London show. Conor was spotted grinning from ear to ear as he held up a pink throng in front of an adoring crowd. The saucy presents, and there were many, began when he performed the song 'Pictures'. In fact he was deluged with so much underwear that his tour manager was forced to clear it all away.

Conor also played in his hometown of Brighton, tweeting: 'Performing at The Dome in Brighton tonight...gonna be crazyyyyy. The calm before the storm...#BrightonDome #ConorTour http://instagr.am/p/RLPS6lj—s/Brighton you were insaneeeee!!!! Thank you so much for an amazing night...x'

TheLatest.co.uk observed: 'If the British music industry was looking out for a home-grown Bieber clone, they landed something rather more sophisticated in Brighton's Conor Maynard. Opening his first tour since debut album *Contrast* shot to number one, Maynard pumped out a floor-rattling mix of upbeat R&B, the smitten crowd screaming the roof down throughout. A welcome acoustic interlude harked back to his early YouTube performances; the version of Nicki Minaj's "Starships" showing his voice can genuinely cut it live. Maynard seemed occasionally overwhelmed at where he's found himself, but this classy, energetic gig proved why he's earned his place at the top.'

As the festive season drew in, Conor found himself besieged with offers of work. On 17 November 2012, he turned on the Christmas lights at Bluewater Shopping Centre in Greenhithe, Kent after being greeted by thousands of screaming fans.

Conor is also a regular at big events and awards shows. On 10 December 2012, he performed at the annual Capital FM Jingle Bell Ball, sharing the bill with some of pop music's biggest names including Pink, Rita Ora, The Wanted and the then newly reunited Girls Aloud.

The cheeky pop star told *Yahoo! OMG!* that he wanted Cheryl Cole in his dressing room as part of his rider, but joked to them on the red carpet at the event: 'I didn't [get Cheryl Cole], no. I got in there and there was bananas, though, and a couple of apples and a passion fruit.

'But it wasn't a passion fruit, it was actually a fig. My tour manager told me it was a passion fruit and I embarrassed myself because I had a big meet and greet in my dressing room and I tried to show off that I knew what fruit it was. But it wasn't, it was a fig.'

During the hit-packed set, he performed 'Contrast', 'Can't Say No', 'Vegas Girl' and 'Turn Around'.

Earlier he had tweeted: 'Performing at Bluewater, switching on Christmas lights, then off to Mayfair Hotel and Mahiki to partyyyyyyy! Crazy day.'

He said he was looking forward to Christmas, adding in an interview: 'This is the first year where I've got money to spend on my family at Christmas. I'm looking forward to treating them. For me, the main thing is getting to see them. I haven't seen them in a while, so it's going to be cool to see them over the Christmas period.'

He often goes back to his hometown to see his family, and he certainly wouldn't miss Christmas day at home for anything – although it would mean an early wake-up call for the no doubt tired pop star. His young sister Anna insists on bouncing on his bed on the festive day in a bid to wake him up – and subsequently get to open her presents earlier.

When asked what he would like for Christmas 2012 by *CraveOnMusic*, he said: 'I want to see my family, I haven't seen them in a long time. Also, I want a car, a Ferrari! Will you get me one?'

He also added that he once nearly set the house on fire when his Christmas stocking caught fire after he put it over the fireplace.

Conor spent time at home during the festive period and seemed to enjoy himself. He wrote: 'Ice skating today! Getting in the Christmas spirit! if falling over repeatedly and crying is the Christmas spirit.'

And he kept fans updated via his tweets: 'Merry Christmas Everyone! I hope you're all spending it with people you care about most, have an amazing day x.' Also, 'Christmas was going so well...we were joking around, laughing, playing games, everything was perfect then I saw a sprout on my plate. Hope you all had an amazing Christmas, I beat my family at Uno Extreme twice so I'm currently feeling like a BOSS.'

He had another reason to celebrate, too. As he explained on Twitter: 'I'm gonna be performing on Top Of The Pops Christmas today btw so make sure you tune in if you'd like!! BBC 1 at 2pm !!'

And he made sure to thank the fans, writing: '2 hours until Christmas!! Make a toast #Mayniacs!! #MyMayniacToastIs to all my amazing fans that have supported me so far... Thank You!!! <3.'

During the show, Conor hooked up with a fellow performer in an attempt to land a future collaboration – Emeli Sandé. He told the *Daily Star*: 'While we were doing the Christmas *Top of the Pops* show, we were saying we'd have to get in the studio together early this year, so I'm very excited about that. It's very cool. When we are back in the UK, it will happen.'

They had known each other for two years, with Conor explaining: 'The first ever Brit [Awards] I went to was with Emeli. We shared a car. Neither of us were known. For me it is a weird feeling, two years down the line, now with all this huge success. This year will be one of the first times I've attended the Brits where people actually know who I am.'

Top of the Pops wasn't the only TV milestone that he seized with both hands, however. The young singer also appeared on BBC1's *Blue Peter*, for decades the enduring staple of kids' TV. Smartly dressed, with a natty quiff in tow, he seemed delighted to be on the iconic show and was soon showing off the *Blue Peter* badge that he received on the show to his fans via Twitter.

2012 was always going to be a busy year for Conor, and it closed with great news. On 30 December, he was delighted to land one million Twitter followers, leading to the release of a YouTube video of him and Anth dancing among others in celebration.

It was particularly apt that Conor was there with Anth to celebrate the news, especially as Anth had been there in the early stages when Conor was trying to make a name for himself on the internet.

In another apt moment, Conor ended 2012 pretty much as he had begun the year – on MTV.

He performed at MTV's New Year's Eve Party: Club NYE in New York.

Delighted to be there, he tweeted: 'Start spreading the news (doo doo doo doo), I'm leaving today (doo doo doo doo), I wanna be a part of it... NEW YORK, NEW YOOORRRK!!' He later tweeted: '30 minutes trying to hail a cab. We pissed! But we in NYC so yaaaay.'

But it was clear that he had thoroughly enjoyed his time in Brighton during the festive period. Hours before jetting off to The Big Apple, he wrote on his Twitter page: 'Conor Maynard @ConorMaynard Gonna miss you Brighton...'

He had someone close to him on the night, admitting to the *Metro*: 'I had a date on New Year's funny enough, when I performed in New York. She's an American lady. People will have maybe seen her in one of my music videos, but I can't really say which one.

'It was fun, it was really cool – I definitely meet people where I feel like going out on a date or something, but nothing serious'.

Showing that he hadn't forgotten his roots, Conor played at a show that was part of MTV's Brand New For 2013. Joining him at London's Forum in Kentish Town on 22 January were the year's nominees, Gabrielle Aplin and Little

Nikki. The gig was announced in December 2012 and Gabrielle said in a statement: 'I'm so excited to have been chosen for MTV Brand New For 2013.

'Lana Del Rey and Lianne La Havas are two of my favourite artists of 2012 and I'm excited to be named as someone who could follow in their footsteps.'

Nikki added: 'This is sick! I've spent my whole life watching music TV so to be part of MTV's Brand New List For 2013 is amazing – I'm gonna go HARD in 2013.'

MusicNews.com wrote: '[When] headliner Conor finally graced the stage he was greeted with the most amount of high pitched girly shrieking and screaming I have ever heard. Mostly coming from the man behind of me. The ladies (and some of the men) lapped up his set. The girls at the front completely lost it and hurled their bras at the poor boy; he was gentlemanly enough to overlook these moments of insanity, and continue to thrill the audience by performing "Vegas Girl" and "Turn Around".

'His wonderfully smooth voice was amazing and I really loved the covers he did. For a minute, I thought it was rather abruptly over, Conor had run off stage and the music finished. Alas fear not,

Conor was only teasing us! After about 20 seconds of the audience cheering his name he came back on stage to finish the set with his debut "Can't Say No".'

The *Observer*'s review of the gig was mixed: 'Maynard, his wearyingly professional four-man band, photographers, cameramen, security guards – and on the other girls, holding handmade signs that say things such as "Animal" and "Vegas Girl" (Maynard singles); some are wearing light-up, hen-night bunny ears. When the girls scream at him your gums hurt. But you do see why they do it: Maynard is a rather better act than this over-familiar scenario of teen pop mania suggests.'

They continued: 'Kicking off a well-drilled set, "Animal" (expected to chart around number four today) tracks Maynard's (quite good) original album version more closely than the (even edgier) remixed single, which features a curveball guest spot from grime MC Wiley. Three songs in, meanwhile, "Vegas Girl" remains a killer urban-lite tune that deserved far better than the number four spot it earned last summer. Lyrically and physically, this 20 nothing from Brighton still toes a fine line between the open sexuality of US R&B and the boy-next-door sensibility of UK teen-pop, wiggling his pelvis coquettishly, air-punching the beats unostentatiously; underlining a pleasurable affinity with 90s-era Justin Timberlake, rather than his fellow youthful YouTube sensation Justin Bieber. During a ballad interlude in which stools replace bras on the stage, Maynard performs an acoustic cover of Nicki Minaj's "Starships" that falls a little flat, reminding you of his origins as a humble uploader of YouTube cover versions.'

Conor also has aspirations to be a music judge. In August 2012, the BBC's talent show *The Voice* was being blasted by critics and losing viewers. However, Conor defended the then beleaguered show, insisting *The Voice*'s judges Jessie J, Tom Jones and Script's Danny O'Donoghue were established singers and insisted it was more credible than ITV talent rival *The X Factor*.

While defending the show, he also put himself in the frame to sit in one of the judging chairs. He said: '*The Voice* was good because it was musicians judging it. With previous pop shows, you'd always hear fans moan, "They're not musicians, so how can they judge it?" But on *The Voice*, the judges know what the people auditioning are going through.'

He added: 'It looks like a fun thing to do, so it's part of the plan to eventually try that sort of thing.

I wouldn't be deliberately brutal as a judge but I'd certainly be honest.'

After the finale of season one of *The Voice*, Conor had befriended Danny O'Donoghue. He said: 'I love The Script but Danny didn't recognise me at first. He asked what I did and I told him I'd sung "Can't Say No".

'Danny worked with Pharrell when he was 19, too, which was a weird coincidence.'

Conor also appeared on *The X Factor* spin-off, *Xtra Factor*. Of the eventual winner James Arthur, he said: 'I haven't had a working TV in over a month. I was on *Xtra Factor* the other day, though, so that was really cool.

'I think James Arthur is up there for me as one of my favourites – he's kind of rocky, a more husky kind of sound. I think he's really cool.'

When asked if he thought James could win, he said: 'I think it's always about moments. I think if someone goes out there and does something incredible, it can switch up everything and sometimes the people that are more like the dark horse do something one of the weeks that is incredible.'

Despite his celebrity status, Conor is still a family boy at heart, saying: 'My family and friends still treat me as the same idiot I was before, so they'll help me keep my feet on the ground. It's all exciting and I'm looking forward to it all. I'm definitely ready to take it and run with it.'

His busy schedule has meant that he has missed out on partying with his old friends, though. He said: 'I do get texts saying, "What's going on? Have you forgotten about me? It's been ages – you said you weren't going to change!" They think I'm so caught up in everything that I forget them, so the difficult part is making them realise that I do think about them, I just don't always have the time to get in touch.'

The fourth single from the album was 'Animal' and Conor was delighted about releasing the song as he was always a huge fan of the track. He remarked: 'Yes, the next single, "Animal", is now featuring Wiley! "Animal" has always been one of my favourite tracks. The album version came out featuring just me – it's a cool remix that we decided to go with for the single. I'm very excited about it; hopefully people will like it! It's slightly different, and shows a more darker, urban side of my music.'

As it was a more mature track with an edgier urban sound, Conor didn't want to release it following the success of 'Can't Say No' and so he decided to wait a little bit.

On meeting Wiley, he said: 'I actually met him at the V Festival. When I saw him for the first time, he just said, "Let's get in the studio, let's do something." So I was like, "Alright, let's do it!" I didn't realise he was going to remix one of my upcoming singles. I thought we were going to get in the studio and work on something new, but the fact that he did that was really cool. It added a whole new urban edge to the track.'

Digital Spy had marked the single out as one to watch at the end of 2011, and a year on they were of the same view. Giving it four out of five stars, they said of Conor's fourth single: 'Despite his sex-charged pleas to "mess me up" being at odds with his boyish charm, 12 months on we're still standing by our judgement that Conor is one of pop's most exciting new stars.'

Other critics weren't so impressed, though. *NME* wrote: 'There's an episode of *The Simpsons* where Bart leads a trip to Shelbyville to recapture Springfield's famous Lemon Tree. On the mission, flouncing nerd Martin is paired with arch-bully Nelson, who reluctantly finds himself having to provide muscular protection for his weedy companion. This is how I imagine Wiley feels about Maynard on this track. It needs less of Maynard and a lot more Wiley.'

Flow of Music also stated: 'It's not special, but I must say that Conor Maynard has a good voice. I hate to use this expression, but this song is too "Mainstream", and I know that I sound like a hipster. This song doesn't stand out from the rest, but it is a little catchy. I would like to see Conor take a new direction, and I would like for him to show some new sides of himself just like he did on "Turn Around". I know that you like to f*ck girls by now, so now I want to see something new. I see less potential in Conor than I see in Justin Bieber, and that says a lot. He's not special.'

Talking about 'Animal' to *Glamour Magazine*, Conor said: 'It's the opening track to the album, and it's a very upbeat song, very kind of crazy, and I love the beat behind it. It's very urban and very cool. And I love the concept of it. It's basically about a girl who can tear you apart, which is a cool idea to go on.'

The song had a darker and sophisticated feel to it, and it was apt that this was his first song of 2013 – hinting at an edgier sound for the coming year. He was now a fully-fledged pop star, performing with high energy, dancing like a pro – he had the whole package.

The video for 'Animal' was set in an abandoned warehouse and in a behind-the-scenes shoot. In a preview, Conor said: 'It's pretty crazy, but I don't want to give too much away.' However, he admitted working with Wiley on the video was 'really fun' and that 'the vibe to the video was pretty crazy'.

On Conor's birthday, the busy pop star couldn't rest for the day to celebrate the special occasion. Instead, he had to work on the second day of the video shoot. However, the crew did their best to ensure that he enjoyed his big day, treating him to cards and presents, including a harmonica. Conor clearly appreciated the gift, playing some tunes in between takes.

As the shoot progressed, a giant cake was handed to him, as the crew all sang 'Happy Birthday'.

Anth tweeted: 'AHHHH!!!!!!! Happy mothaf*ckin birthday to my BOYYYY / BEST FRIEND / BROTHA FROM ANOTHA MOTHA / MOTHER LOVER @ConorMaynard!!!! Love you man.'

In a series of posts, Conor wrote: 'My last couple of hours as a teenager. what do I do WHAT DO I DO?!

'My year of being 19 has literally been incredible though guys, and I have all you #Mayniacs to thank for that.

'All the amazing support you have all shown and constant faith in me has been amazing.'

'Animal' was another Top 10 hit for Conor, who was now a fully-fledged pop star.

It wasn't all good news, though. Conor thought his London home was haunted, telling *Metro*: 'I'd just moved into my new place and came back to find some of my things had been moved. I thought there might have been someone in my house. It was a bit strange. Then, one day, I walked into my room and there was a cat sitting there. I then realised it had been coming in through the cat flap the previous owner had put in. So my stuff hadn't been moved around by a ghost, it was being done by a cat.'

Conor likes to while away any down time from becoming a pop sensation by watching chick flicks. Dubbing it his guilty pleasure, his personal favourite is *John Tucker Must Die*, and he is also addicted to the recent TV remake of *Beverly Hills 90210* – although he revealed that he blames his ex girlfriend for getting him into it.

One thing he hoped to gain from his success was getting his hands on something that eludes many of us and is only given to a chosen few. He's addicted to spicy chicken eatery Nando's and for a while he had his fingers crossed that eventually his celebrity status would land him a prestigious Nando's Black Card. Fortunately for him, it did, and he counts it as one of his greatest ever successes.

He told *PyroMag.com*: 'Yes, I get the same thing every time I go. I get the Humous Appetiser, then I get a Chicken Wrap with Medium Spice. If I'm really hungry I will get a side with that, drinkwise I will get a Mango Juice, then once I have finished drinking the juice I just fill it up with the fizzy drinks. My goal in life is to get a Nando's Black Card so if I get one of those I don't think anyone will see me ever again. I would hide in Nando's for the rest of my life!'

Conor certainly has an appetite for Nando's. In April 2012, he performed a secret gig at a London branch of the restaurant chain, thrilling lucky fans with a rendition of his then new song 'Can't Say No'.

A Nando's spokesperson said: 'It was an incredible way to show off our latest restaurant. Everyone had an amazing night, thanks to Conor and all the other performers, and of course our Nando's team who kept us all topped up with peri-peri treats.'

And in an interview with *Glamour Magazine* , Conor stated: 'I would like to set up my own house in a Nando's, maybe just buy a tent and set up in

Nando's so I can have Nando's whenever I want.' Then, when asked where he sees himself in five years' time, he said: 'Nah, nah, I don't really know – I think I will definitely be working on music. I don't know which album I'd be on by then, but you know, just carrying on with what I'm doing.'

He added in another interview, this time with *Ink Splot*: 'There is a food chain in the UK called Nando's, and it is my absolute favourite. I actually have the Black Card they hand out and there's only 100 that exist in the entire world, and I have one, and it means that you get it for free. Yeah, that was literally like my pinnacle success so far; that was like a massive moment for me. I also like Chipotle over in the US.'

He added: 'Yes! I think I've used it every day.'

In an old tweet, he said: 'A nandos near me has closed I feel like my world is crumbling around me.'

Another culinary guilty pleasure is Dunkin' Donuts – Conor admits it's his first stop whenever he is in America. It's possible that he needs the extra fuel for he admits that he has to live on cornflakes as he regularly sets off the smoke alarm whenever he tries to cook a steak.

His eating habits were becoming more and more newsworthy, too, with the *Hackney Gazette* running a story about him and his friends enjoying a meal at Thai restaruant Yum Yum on London's Stoke Newington High Street.

The owner of the restaurant, Atique Choudhury, said: 'Conor came to dinner with some friends. He had a fantastic meal. His friends were celebrities and people from the music industry. We got Conor behind the bar and showed him to how to make our signature cocktail Yum Yum Mohito. Afterwards he left to go to Japanese restaurant Oishiii for some karaoke.'

He added: 'It's nice to have people in the music industry coming into restaurants in Hackney. There are lots of artists and celebrities and musicians hanging around in Stoke Newington now. A few weeks ago, 50 Cent came to a barbershop in Stoke Newington to get a facial before his birthday bash in Mayfair. It's a cool place to be.'

Conor's eating habits aren't the only things he asked about – apparently he gets quizzed on his cleaning habits too. When asked what superpower he would have, he said: 'I'd be invisible so I could hide from my managers when they tell me to clean my house.'

Fame still hasn't gone to his head. He drives the same car that he had when he was 17 – a Vauxhall Corsa, which cost just £400. It's been keyed four times, but he still has a huge fondness for his car and has no plans to get rid of it.

He admits that it's been hard to see his friends since basking in pop glory, but insists he's still grounded: 'I'm crazily busy and I'm always in other countries meeting new people so it gets a bit hard to see my friends at home. I like to surround myself by people I've known from the beginning to keep grounded and humble.

'My dad is a builder and my mum works in an office, so maybe the way I've been brought up will keep me there.'

In fact, Conor has said he would most likely be at university if his career hadn't taken off as it did. Indeed, such is his humility that he has spoken of his occasional jealousy of his friends at university, saying: 'I look at my friends in uni and think it would have been really fun to go to uni.'

While Conor remains grounded, he still has plenty of celebrity friends, including Jessie J, Tulisa and Tinie Tempah.

He joked about Tinchy Stryder, saying: 'Tinchy is definitely Tiny, but even though he is small, he could still beat me up if I told him that to his face. I know he was at the SECC for *In:Demand* but he was playing FIFA the last time I saw him and you never interrupt a guy who is playing FIFA.'

He's still looking for romance, too. A keen romantic at heart, Conor admitted to *Reveal magazine*: 'I'm single and ready to mingle. I don't have the time to give a girl what she deserves because things are crazy right now. I'm focused on getting where I want to be. But, in a relationship, I like to go one step further. One ex-girlfriend really wanted to see a West End show in London, so I booked tickets, then arranged for her to stay at a five-star hotel as well. She was really excited.'

However, the singer can never really fully switch off from music. Typical of someone who hasn't forgotten his roots, he enjoys spending a night off watching music videos from new artists on YouTube. Despite acknowledging that thanks to his success, and that of Justin Bieber, it's harder to get noticed now that so many people have tried to emulate them, he still believes it's a brilliant platform for young musicians.

He's constantly thinking of new music for his album and is not averse to making up an impromptu recording studio while on his travels. However, he nearly got into trouble on one occasion after setting up a temporary studio at Glasgow's Crowne Plaza in 2012.

He told the *Daily Record*: 'The producers behind "Can't Say No" and "Vegas Girl" came to my hotel room to do a session with singer/songwriter Ms D. Schedules are so tight and there are not any days off before America so we've had to do some writing and recording on the road.

'We were blasting songs and trying to get a vibe when there was a knock on the door from hotel security, asking us to turn it down. We recorded for two hours from 10.45am to 12.45pm but they still asked us to turn it down.'

He added: 'I'm kind of recording new music all the time. Before this interview, I was in a room along the corridor with a bunch of producers that worked on my first album. I'm always working on upcoming projects.'

Conor has also become a regular figure on the small screen, appearing on panel shows, including *Celebrity Juice* and *Never Mind the Buzzcocks*. He told *TheYorker.co.uk*: 'I was pretty nervous to do it but the day before I had recorded *Never Mind the Buzzcocks* so I was in that panel show mode anyway. I was so nervous for *Buzzcocks*, it was my first ever one and they're all really clever and witty on the show, and then there's just me. I could tell as soon as I sat down that I was in the "abused pop star chair" but I was quite lucky 'cos we all got on well.

'For *Celebrity Juice* it was really fun. I got to

meet Keith Lemon before the show and he was really nice – I was worried he would just be horrible and see me as just a young pop star, but because I got a chance to meet him, he got to see that I'm not the really arrogant kind of guy that would try and be really cool.'

On appearing on *Celebrity Juice*, he added: 'I can't believe my parents actually watched that! I put up a status on Facebook to all my friends saying, "I'm going to be on *Celebrity Juice* tonight, Mum please don't watch!" She wasn't actually going to watch but then she kept getting phone calls about it, so she ended up watching it with my dad, and now they want to disown me.'

Since his success, Conor has made several purchases, including baseball caps. However, he has stopped wearing them because of internet rumours that he has gone bald. He told the *Daily Star*: 'I have about 50 hats but stopped wearing them because of rumours I was bald! I thought, "I'm 20 and people think I'm bald? It's time to ban them!"'

Altogether, he has owned over a hundred pairs of trainers, admitting: 'My dad made me count all my trainers and I had about 127 pairs.' Of his hectic schedule, he added: 'I'm going to see my friends less and less because of work but I won't ever forget them. In one of Drake's songs he talks about taking his friends on a massive holiday and paying for it all. I can imagine doing that, taking my friends away on holiday as a thank you for being so patient while I was so busy doing the pop thing.'

Despite his fame, Conor doesn't always hit the nightclubs. He laughed: 'I try to party but I like to sleep more. That's my down time – literally on the floor asleep.'

At the start of 2013, fans of Conor were given a treat. MasterCard teamed up with Conor, Rita Ora and Delilah to allow fans a chance to remake their videos to mark the company's 15th anniversary as a partner of the Brit Awards.

The Priceless Remake competition gave fans an ideal chance to show their directorial abilities. Shaun Springer, head of Brand and Sponsorship at MasterCard UK & Ireland, said: 'Last year, we offered music fans the opportunity to have a priceless duet with their idols. This year, we are going one better and are thrilled to offer MasterCard cardholders the ultimate priceless experience – the chance to actually be their idol for the day and star as them in a music video – as well as joining them at the 2013 Brit Awards.'

He added: 'This is just the start, watch this space

as we will be giving more back to music fans and bringing them closer to the artists they love in the run up to the Brits on *somethingforthefans.co.uk*.'

The winning entrants got the chance to shoot a shot-for-shot recreation of the video. The video were directed by regular Rita Ora promo director Emil Nava, and also saw them mingle with the stars at the Brit Awards.

The Brit Awards are one of the biggest musical events in the British calendar. The ceremony is the British Phonographic Industry's Annual Music Awards Show, and was first introduced in 1977 to coincide with the Queen's Silver Jubilee, before becoming an annual event in 1982.

The 2013 ceremony took place at London's O2 Arena on 20 February. The glitzy show saw Emeli Sandé win the Best British Female and British Album categories for her debut album *Our Version Of Events*.

She said at the event: 'This is an album I wrote because I didn't have the confidence to say these things in person.

'For me, that so many people have connected with this album and found strength in these words makes me feel incredible and it doesn't make me feel as lonely.' Singer Ben Howard won the Best British Male and Breakthrough categories – much to a lot of people's surprise. Rita Ora was expected to take the Breakthrough trophy, and no one seemed more shocked than the singer himself. He said: 'Wow, thank you very much. That's bizarre isn't it? I didn't really expect to, erm... I was quite stoked to come to the awards to be honest, so to come away with two of these things is amazing, so thank you all very much.'

Adele won Best Single for the theme to the 2012 James Bond movie *Skyfall*. She couldn't attend the event because she was rehearsing for the Oscars in LA. A good decision in hindsight, as, days later she also won the gold statuette for Best Song.

A video message was played at the Brits, and she couldn't help referring to the previous year's ceremony, which saw her winning speech infamously cut short by producers because the live show had overrun. She said: 'Thank you so much for this Brit Award, it means a lot. Sorry I can't be with you tonight, I'm in LA rehearsing for the Oscars. I won't keep you too long because I don't want to interrupt the best album speech at the end of the night. But I love you all.'

The night was a success but many noted that the show seems to have lost its rock and roll roots.

For years, the show was dominated by controversy, and it didn't feel like the Brits if the front pages weren't dominated the day afterwards with something that had happened at the show. In previous years, we have seen politicians doused with water by anarchic musicians, bitter feuds between musicians and, most famously of all, Michael Jackson's stage performance interrupted by Pulp superstar Jarvis Cocker and his wiggling bum in the 1996 ceremony. Fast forward 17 years and much has changed. The thank you speeches were family friendly, the atmosphere was warm – although One Direction decided to give famous pop-punk anthem 'Teenage Kicks' by The Undertones an edgy makeover by mashing it with Blondie's 'One Way or Another' . The BBC noted: 'It was hardly the most raucous event in the history of rock 'n' roll. And there lies the problem. The Brits want to trumpet the amazing success of British music around the world, but the voters are resolutely conservative.'

Befitting his new fame and status as one of Britain's biggest pop superstars, it wasn't a surprise to see Conor attend the event. The Brits featured minute-long Priceless Remake adverts of videos of their favourite stars, including Conor and Ne-Yo.

Conor told *Yahoo!* about turning up at the shoot for the remake adverts featuring one of the competition winners: 'That was hilarious! He literally had no idea I was going to jump out so he was pretty shocked to say the least. But it was cool, all the extras were there so they added to the vibe – it wasn't awkward or anything – I didn't want to scare him! It was meant to be fun so all the extras were like, "Woah," and he couldn't believe it; it was cool, it was a fun vibe definitely.'

At the red carpet, Conor looked like he was having the time of his life, wearing a suave and sophisticated two-piece suit, white shirt and sneakers. He told journalists: 'It's amazing – it's actually my third Brits. I've been here three years in a row and it's the first year where I've turned up and people actually know who I am and care. This year it's very different and it's fun.'

It was a successful show, attracting a peak audience of 7.3 million viewers. An average 6.5-million viewing audience made it the most watched Brits show since 2003.

Conor found himself on the defence after it was rumoured he was dating former *EastEnders* actress Preeya Kalidas. The 32-year-old was seen holding hands with the young pop star at the Brits after party, according to the *Sun*.

A source told the newspaper: 'Conor didn't really want to be photographed because he doesn't know how things will turn out. He just wants to take things slowly. But he really gets on with her and she's hoping there's a future there.'

While he initially kept quiet about his relationship with the beautiful actress, Conor took to Twitter to say: 'Brits and after parties were GREAT!!! Which is why it took me until 8pm to tweet about them… or tweet anything. Hahaaa.'

However, Preeya also took to Twitter, denying their relationship. She wrote: 'It's not true. It's ridiculous.'

And Connor added, days later: 'Guys! The story about me dating @PreeyaKalidas isn't true. She's a lovely friend but that's all :) I'm still single and ready to mingle :D'.

In his spare time, Conor likes to keep fit, telling the *Telegraph*: 'If I have a late night, I could stay in bed until the afternoon, but I don't usually have a choice – my days are planned. At the beginning of last year I had a personal trainer, who would call me at 6am to make sure I was out of bed – he was an ex-Army guy.'

And when asked about his style, he added to the *Telegraph*: 'Fittings are boring, but it's fun when you get to wear something new and go to a new event. I have a massive say in what I wear – I work really closely with my stylist. I love my Kooples jeans, Adidas and Nike trainers – I've got 150 pairs of trainers – and All Saints T-shirts. I'm given a lot of clothes – that's one of the things my friends are most jealous of.'

His stylist, Cobi Yates, told *Mr Porter.com*: 'He's at a moment of transition now. He's developing as an artist, his fan base is growing with him, and he's moving from that colourful, youthful look to a smarter, more adult style while still staying true to his roots.'

And Conor is also learning how to deal with the paparazzi, telling *Rolling Stone*: 'You've just got to know what you're doing. You've got to sit back and realise that because of what we do, what artists do, they're interested in what you're doing. You've got to be conscious of that. You've got to realize that this is your life and that's the consequence I have to pay for all the amazing things I've achieved. You have to find that balance.'

He added: 'With incredible names like Pharrell and Frank Ocean on my album, they're so respected for their music, first and foremost. I feel like that's the kind of thing I'm going for. I want people to respect me for the voice I have and the music I have to give. Whether that means paparazzi chasing me around, I don't know. But as long as there are people out there listening to and enjoying my music, I'm happy.'

At Capital's Jingle Bell Ball in December 2012, Conor said: 'I'm working on new stuff right now. I've been in New York doing more with Ne-Yo, more writing. I'm going to be doing a good session next year. Don't know if I'm allowed to say too much about it yet, but definitely VERY exciting!'

Days later, he tweeted: 'I so badly want you guys to hear the song I'm recording right now...Maybe I should tease you with some lyrics...Don't stop to breathe, just give me everything...'

CHAPTER SEVEN

NEXT STOP, AMERICA

After *Contrast* topped the British album charts, there was little room for celebration, as talk immediately turned to launching it across the globe, with all eyes on one particular market.

'The US was definitely one of the main targets for me,' Conor told Clevver TV.

He seemed to have timed it perfectly. British acts were enjoying a great time in the US charts, with Americans in love with acts such as One Direction, Adele and Mumford & Sons. One Direction in particular have enjoyed huge success, scoring two number one albums and enjoying the sort of crowd mania that echoed Beatlemania and the early days of The Rolling Stones.

And with Conor's music perfectly suited to American pop urban fans, thanks to the polished production on his album and big name collaborations, the young singer was hopeful. Speaking to *Yahoo! OMG!* he said: 'It's crazy, I think for me it's cool that so many British artists were put together and this amazing story of success has followed. There are so many Brits being recognised right now and it's amazing. Obviously, they [Americans] all think I sound like Harry Potter, which is kind of weird!'

'But I think that when I pass by these artists it's cool that we are flying the flag out there right now, it's a lot of fun. I feel like I definitely want to keep focused on the music because it's taking me so many places.

'I bumped into a few guys when I was out there. I bumped into Rita [Ora], Ed Sheeran, Ellie Goulding – a whole bunch of us.'

He told *Maximum Pop*: 'I do want to break America! It's quite scary, it is a big place to try and break. It's an amazing place, but for me I don't think I could live anywhere other than the UK. I love my home too much but then again, I am only

19 so I haven't really been able to experience America properly.'

Rohan Blair-Mangat, director of 'Can't Say No', told this author: 'It's hard to say how big he will become. When I was first approached to direct his video I had never heard of him before. As a British pop and RnB record, I thought this has serious production values. It sounded like an American track, and not a standard British track. Even then, when I was working with him, he was telling me that Pharrell [Williams] had reached out to him. He sounded surprised that he was heading out to America to work with him. When you know people like that are involved then you know he's definitely going to be huge. I know he's massive in Britain, but it wouldn't surprise me at all if he becomes massive there. He told me that when he was making the videos in the bedroom he was always watching other videos to see how they did it, and whether he could match it with the technology he had learned while making them.'

In July 2012, Conor appeared in New York for a showcase: The Gallery at Dream Hotel. It was an event that saw him perform in front of the Mayniacs and selected media figures. Such showcases, in front of jaded industry types, more often than not lack the fizzle of a normal concert. But with the Mayniacs in tow, armed with hats that had 'Vegas Girl' emblazoned on them, thanks to canny EMI music bods, the occasion was guaranteed to have plenty of fizz. Conor managed to calm his nerves, kicking off the show with 'Animal', and made sure to thank his fans for all their support over the last couple of years.

By this stage, he was becoming increasingly confident on stage, reasoning: 'I feel like performing is probably one of my favourite parts of being an artist and kind of like, vibing off the audience and the energy when you're performing. Drawing them in when you do a slow song and making them jump around when you're doing a crazy song – I think it's a really cool vibe.'

In September 2012, he observed to *The Magazine*: 'Obviously there are British artists that are big in the UK and not big over here, and it's different in that sense. But then, we listen to a lot of North American music over in the UK – I suppose that's why it's a dream of most artists to break over here because everyone follows the sound that comes through here. But there's a massive eye on British talent right now, so it's an amazing time for me to be releasing my stuff and I'm really excited about it.'

He added: 'American fans are pretty insane. They like to chase me and follow me and scream.'

Conor also notes how US fans are different to his home-grown ones, adding: 'It's kind of crazy in the US because in their heads, all the certain places I go to with the fans, they think I'm never going to come back there again because I've been to so many random parts of America. So they try to make the most of each moment that they meet me. I'll do a signing and they'll turn up with muffins and doughnuts. It would be cool if one of them gave them to me but all of them give them to me, and I'm like, "OK I'm going to become morbidly obese if I carry on!"'

As an ordinary boy from Brighton, he was overjoyed to have been let loose in America. For the singer, who had been raised on a diet of American music, video games and films while growing up, it was a dream come true. It wasn't all plain sailing, however – he was left red-faced after he lost his passport.

He tweeted: 'Lost my passport while I'm in America. This is not ideal. You know that when all the trending topics are in a different language...it's time for bed.'

As promotion heated up for the debut of his album, Conor made sure to indulge in some perks, including sitting in amazing seats to watch his very first baseball game: New York Knicks versus the Boston Celtics at the iconic Madison Square Garden.

Conor still does covers, and the canny self-publicist completed another one to celebrate the New Year and his bid to crack America. He tweeted: 'To celebrate the release of my album in the US, I'm going to be putting up a new cover on YouTube on the 8th, so I hope you're excited! I do have the new cover ready to upload today...just need you US #Mayniacs to keep pushing the album before I upload the cover!! :)'

A few hours later in a series of Twitter posts, he added: 'Mmmmm a lucky few of you got to hear the new cover early :) I've made a proper video for it though, you guys think you're ready...?

'Ok, if you think you're ready for this new cover, imma need you guys to trend something for me...Ok the next tweet will be the one I need you to RT like crazy, and keep RT'ing the hashtag!!!'

Chart glory in America would bring him one step closer towards his dream meeting with superstar Drake. He told *MTV News*: 'I went through a massive phase of just listening to Drake's music. I was just a massive fan of his music, and the way he writes is just incredible. He makes such simple, relatable tracks that work so cleverly. It's so weird how he writes.

'If I ever got the chance to work with him or got to meet him, I think it would be one of those moments where it's like, "Don't cry, don't cry, don't cry!" It would be crazy. I definitely look up to him as an artist.'

In October 2012, he began to make a splash in New York by having a blue bus – boldly emblazoned with 'Conor' on the side – proclaiming 'The British Pop Sensation – Conor Maynard'. Fans were urged to hop on.

Conor said of 'The Mayniac Express': 'It's been crazy here in New York. The fans have been amazing.

'It's like a dream come true at the moment.'

He appeared on *The Today Show*, saying: 'It was insane to do that – my first time performing on television in America. I got the chance to chill with my fans on a bus – the Mayniac bus, which has my face on it so it's the best bus ever! And it gave the fans a chance to be really creative because they had to make the best poster to get on the bus.'

In a coup for the youngster, he appeared on the iconic chat show, *The Late Show*, to perform a song at the start of 2013. It was arguably his most nerve-wracking and important show.

He tweeted: 'Performing on David Letterman @Late_Show tonight! Check it out if you like x'

Holding a copy of his album, veteran entertainment host David Letterman said: 'Our next guest is a talented singer and songwriter. This is his debut CD. It went to number one in his native England, entitled *Contrast*. Ladies and gentleman, please welcome Conor Maynard.'

Clad mainly in black, Conor looked completely at ease as he stalked the dance floor, emoting furiously as he sang 'Turn Around' – much to the delight of the millions watching. Shouting to the audience, 'Here we go!' before the chorus, he launched into an energetic performance, complete with some dad-style dancing and jumping around the stage. The performance was all the more impressive considering the size of the audience and the pressure he must have faced.

As the song ended, he smiled thinly and the crowd burst into applause. Letterman appeared on stage to congratulate the young singer and warmly thanked him and the audience as the show came to a close.

Conor has a firm hand on how to tease his supporters, saying: 'Btw to celebrate the release of my album in the US, I'm going to be putting up a new cover on YouTube on the 8th, so I hope you're excited! Before adding to determine how early in the day I release the cover, tweet me as MANY screenshots as possible showing me you've pre-ordered the album!!'

Following his *The Late Show* appearance, the young Brit scarcely had time to settle as he was suddenly thrown into appearing on another iconic TV show, *Good Morning America*. He tweeted: 'Gonna be performing on Good Morning America in about 15 minutes. Tune in! Make sure you watch it, if I have to be up that early, so do you. Hahaaa.'

USA Today gave him an impressive three out of four rating, reasoning: 'Whether you think the third British Invasion started with Adele or One Direction, it's hard not to see Conor Maynard as its latest front. Pharrell and Rita Ora are guests here as well, and Frank Ocean co-writes one of the album's highlights, the falsetto-tinged *Pictures*. Given Maynard's age and back-story, comparisons to Justin Bieber are inevitable, but *Contrast* suggests he'll outgrow them.'

The *San Francisco Chronicle* noted: 'Although it would be easy to mistake 19-year-old Conor Maynard for a wayward member of One Direction, he's more likely Britain's belated answer to Justin Bieber. Like his Canadian counterpart, he was discovered when his self-made YouTube videos, in which he covered songs by Drake and Katy Perry, drew millions of viewers. He also roped in an expensive cadre of R&B producers to give his breathy, wide-eyed pop tunes serious lustre on his debut album, *Contrast*. Collaborators such as Stargate, Pharrell Williams and Frank Ocean work their usual magic – the high-energy Ne-Yo duet "Turn Around" and wobbly M.I.A. tribute "Can't Say No" feel like future chart conquerors – while Maynard's primary directive seems to be to stay the hell out of the way.'

Again, comparisons were to be made with Justin Bieber, with Conor telling *MTV News*: 'I don't want to be the next anyone. I want to be the first Conor Maynard. I think I want to have a successful career that is unique in its own way.'

Meanwhile, *JournalSentinel.com* observed: 'Maynard is no mere copycat. His debut album is less ambitious than Bieber's latest, "Believe", with its EDM-infused, arena-worthy anthems. Yet Maynard has a more mature, soulful voice than Bieber, and a more adult pop sound than his fellow countrymen in One Direction. Maynard holds his own with Ne-Yo on "Turn Around" and achieves some smooth, Maxwell-style falsetto flourishes on

"Pictures". And while *Contrast* ends with the two dullest tracks, the Pharrell-penned-and-produced "Glass Girl" and "Just in Case", *Contrast*, with its peppy production work on the other tracks – primarily from U.K. trio The Invisible Men – is flirty and fun.'

And the influential *Rolling Stone* wrote: 'Angel-faced Conor Maynard has been called the "British Bieber", though at age 20, the Brighton, England native is a greybeard next to his Canadian counterpart. Like Bieber, Maynard was discovered after posting cover songs on YouTube and mentored by an established star (Ne-Yo). On his debut, a chart-topping smash in the U.K., he displays a Bieber-like flair for mixing boy-band guilelessness with state-of-the-art R&B style. Maynard doesn't quite put a personal stamp on catchy, generic tracks like "Animal" or "Can't Say No", or convince as a lothario. Still, the songs are good, and he can sing. On the Frank Ocean co-write "Pictures", he flashes a falsetto that recalls another Justin: Timberlake.'

Not content with his early success, Conor is still looking to improve, reasoning: 'I want to work with singer/songwriters. I'm hoping to work with Ed Sheeran or John Mayer. The first album was very much about the big up-tempo numbers and now it's time to get into something a bit more intimate and acoustic to really show my voice. I'm not going to move away completely from the upbeat songs as I love doing them but I'd love to try some new stuff. You've got to experiment, don't you?'

And in another interview, he added to *The Student Pocket Guide*: 'I'm probably going to spend a lot of time in America; my album comes out in January over there so I'll be doing a lot of work. I'm going to be working on new music; I'm actually now working on some new stuff for upcoming singles and albums. So yeah, I think I'm just going to continue working on new music, doing different shows, and hopefully another tour so I can come back here, which would be really cool!'

The debut album ultimately peaked at number 34 in the hard-to-break US charts. It was a respectful first position and one that he will no doubt wish to better with further albums.

Conor also has another goal in mind: 'I love acting in front of a camera. I would love to go back to acting again, but I've got to get the music done first. It's been good for the music videos and performing onstage.'

He added to the *Daily Star*: 'I acted at college and have had some random offers come in, but it's too soon to consider them.'

CHAPTER EIGHT

THE MAYNIACS

Every pop star has a fan base, but not all stars have a special name for their fans. However, Lady Gaga has her 'Little Monsters', while Justin Bieber has his 'Beliebers' and Conor Maynard has his 'Mayniacs'.

Conor told the *Telegraph*: 'My fans are called Mayniacs. They enjoy screaming and chasing me and taking pictures, they do crazy things. I've got a cool connection with them through Twitter and Facebook. They use all the words that I use; it's crazy, it's like I actually influence what they say and think.'

They are dubbed 'The Mayniacs', a phrase coined by Conor and his fans after realising that a lot of celebrities have names for their fans. Conor said: 'I gotta have one. I gotta jump in on this,' and so he tweeted the fans to help him come up with a name. It ended up being a two-way choice between 'Mayniacs' and 'Condom' – a saucy term similar to Conor Kingdom.

He later admitted, however: 'The annoying thing was I forgot who tweeted it initially! I told everyone they were called Mayniacs and this girl tweeted me saying, "I can't believe you stole my idea. You didn't even credit me for it, I'm no longer a Mayniac!" But I quickly gave her a shout out and she said she loved me again!'

Conor told *Just Jared* that there could have been more of a risky name: 'All these stupid ideas came through, and it ended up being between the Mayniacs and the Condoms. That was the other idea: The Conor Condoms. So, yeah, I went with the Mayniacs. I didn't feel like walking out into a venue and being like, "What's up condoms?!"'

While it may be hard to believe now, Conor wasn't always a hit with the opposite sex. In fact, his mum was there to pick him up after a failed romance. He told the *Daily Mail*: 'When I was 13, I remember crying on my mum's shoulder when my first girlfriend dumped me via MSN Messenger.'

And when asked what type of girl he is looking for, he replied: 'I don't really know because looking at my past relationships growing up there hasn't really been a common thing between all of the girls – they have all been very different. For me it is more about the connection you have with that girl rather than what they look like. I look for a good connection – like, if we have the same sense of humour and we like the same sorts of things.'

With his boyish charm and mischievous smile it's no surprise that Conor has a sizeable fan base. His teen idol looks come at a price, however. He told Britain's *Celebs on Sunday magazine*: '[I get ID'd for alcohol] all the time. I can't get anywhere without ID. On my 18th birthday I was escorted out of Sainsbury's [supermarket] for getting annoyed at the cashier. They wouldn't sell me a certificate-15 video game because I didn't have ID on me. They thought I looked 14 on my 18th birthday.'

Whether buying him packets of wine gums because his surname is similar to that of a famous British confectionary brand, or professing their love for him on Twitter, it's clear that when it comes to fans, Conor Maynard's are a different breed. He has had problems with fans, though, and was once forced to leave the family home after an encounter with his rabid fan base.

He told Radio 1 DJ Nick Grimshaw: 'The ones that found my house were those that lived near me. There was six of them. I was buying some milk. One ran, and I thought she wasn't a fan. Then she came back minutes later with 40 more people – they were saying, "Is that your house?" and I was like, "No, it's a friend's." Then they kept knocking. I think when you go home, it's your private time.'

He added in another interview: 'It only takes one person to overstep the line, then they all do. Dublin Airport was ridiculous – I had to get a police escort. One fan just kind of grabbed me, then all of them were chasing, and trying to get pictures and autographs and wouldn't let me go.

'It's all switched. My average trip around the corner to get a pint of milk might include being followed, screamed at, having my song sung at me, pictures being taken. I had to move from my house because fans found out where I lived. Then this morning I found a little note stuck to my door, saying, "I live right across from you, can I get a picture real soon?" So I'll probably have to move again. It's quite funny, really.'

Of his Dublin encounter, he added: 'I was in an airport in Dublin, Ireland and I actually had a police escort through the airport. They had me in a headlock. I was crying in their arms as they were snapping photos. Probably wasn't the best picture!'

One fan in Dublin gave him a gift to remember: 'JLS condom,' he told *We Love Pop*. 'It was really random. I was in Dublin and a fan just came up to me and handed it to me in the box. I was like, "Well, this is a bit weird."'

As someone who was there at the start, Anth Melo knows better than most about Conor's dedicated fan base. He told this author: 'The Mayniacs are... Maniacs. Haha! They definitely live up to the name in every way possible. Whether it comes to chasing you down the block, or crying hysterically when they see you, they'll make sure you know they're Mayniacs, haha. They're also some of the greatest fans you'll ever meet. I love the Mayniacs.'

Conor often gets tweets from his fans asking him to marry them. However, he's discovered the best way to defuse the situation is just by saying: 'Yeah, okay, I will marry you. Let's go!'

He joked: 'They never know what to say to that.' Conor also revealed: 'People turn up to my shows five hours early. I got to one of my shows in London at nine in the morning for a soundcheck – the show was at 2pm – and there were people already there. I was like, "What are you doing here?" They had to get the coach at 3am from Cardiff! I was thinking, "I wouldn't even go that far to see my show!" It was crazy. It's really flattering, though.'

Of Amsterdam, he said: 'I did a show in Amsterdam recently, and the fans did a flash mob. I walked out of the radio station and there was a little group of fans, like five of them. And they were standing there right next to a little CD player. And I was like, "What's going on here?" They pressed the CD and "Turn Around" started playing. And about 60 fans jumped out of bushes and they all started dancing; they had these routines planned out and they just did it.'

There are some cheekier fans, however. The then teenage singer was stunned when one fan told him that her baby was conceived to one of his songs.

'It's nice to know I cause pregnancy,' he joked.

But he was shocked when the stage was covered in condoms at a recent show in Canada, telling the *Sunday Mirror*: 'The crowd wouldn't stop throwing them and I kept slipping over – I'm scarred for life.' He continued: 'It got very manic in Canada, with people ringing up the hotels asking if I was staying there, and so we changed hotels a few times. In the UK, it's got a bit more crazy – to go around the corner to get a pint of milk isn't so easy anymore! I've actually got to move house because some fans found out where I live. Mostly girls, young screaming girls and the odd boy.'

He added: 'I was in a shop earlier this year and a female fan saw me and screamed so loudly that everyone stopped and looked round. It was like someone had died. And the worst thing about it was at that point no one else knew who I was.

'And the girl was with her Nan, who then turned around and started asking everyone who I was.'

Conor loves his fans, though, and showed it through his Mayniac Meet Ups – tweeting a location and meeting any fans that turned up. He did them in America while visiting the country in September and October 2012 – and while mostly fairly low-key events, just signing some things, one particular occasion did get out of hand.

He told the *Guardian*: 'We did one here in a candy store and it went crazy. We had no security and over 200 girls turned up! We got kicked out of the shop.'

In fact, the attention has got so much that Conor

has taken to going out in disguise in a bid to avoid recognition. He told *Now* magazine: 'I wear a disguise so I don't have to fight off girls in the street. I might use a mask or glasses and a big hat. Sometimes it doesn't work and I do get chased.

'It's kind of crazy how my fans will come to the show and they'll literally wait outside till about 2 or 3am. When we actually leave and get ready to go, they'll still be outside waiting for a picture or an autograph, so it is very insane.'

And he also admitted he would react with fear if he found a female fan in his hotel room. He said: 'I'd probably just run. I think if they've broken into my room, I wouldn't be very welcoming. I think I'd probably just be really scared and start crying. I'd find my manager or security and get someone to save my life!'

And the tour bus is definitely a no-go area for female fans. Conor told *BANG showbiz*: 'If I invited ladies onto the bus, it would be so cramped and none of us would be able to move. It would be a bit of a vibe killer if I met a girl and made her come on to the bus.

'Also, we're all guys on there so it's just kind of got beer and stuff all around. It's not really the most welcoming place to walk into, so I wouldn't really bring a girl to the bus if I met a girl. I think she'd probably run away and never speak to me again.'

During his stage appearances, Conor was inundated with fans throwing underwear at him. He admitted: 'When it hits you in the face, it kind of puts you off. But when it just lands on the stage, it's one of those things where you just ignore it and continue.

'I think I got hit in the face by a scarf at the show in Manchester. It actually kind of knocked me sideways so I couldn't even continue singing for a second. I had to kind of readjust myself.'

He also revealed: 'One time after a show, the fans kind of created a human ladder up the window, to the dressing room.'

And it's not only teenage girls who have fallen for Conor's charms and his music. He said: 'A fair share of mums do turn up at my shows. If I met someone and there was a connection, their age wouldn't make a difference. Unless it was ridiculous, and she was in her 70s.'

After being told that Katie Price is a Mayniac, he remarked: 'Don't get me wrong, if I bumped into her in a club and she was friendly, I'd talk to her and party with her. She's probably a fun person to party with.'

Eventually, he met her while working on the TV

show *Celebrity Juice*, saying: 'We actually had something to speak about. She's spent a lot of time in Brighton, I'm obviously from there so we had a little chat about it. I think sometimes she gets a bit misread on those kind of shows because she knows what she's going to get, so she builds up this defence. She always says she comes across as rude on TV shows, but she's just trying to defend herself. But she was actually really nice off-camera; she was really cool. A lot of my friends were saying to me, "You should watch out for Katie Price", and I was like, 'Why, what's going to happen?!" but like I said, she was really nice. Haha! She said something that I didn't understand at first! I said to her, "Oh, apparently if I was a bit older" and then she said, "Yeah, you're a sort." I was like, "I have no idea what that means!"'

Of the fans' mums, he said: 'I was walking down the road the other day and a car full of women drove past with the windows down. One of them went, "Is that Conor Maynard?" and another went, "He's so yummy!" I pretended I didn't hear it and kept on walking. It's all fun. There's always something special about cougars. I'm happy being single for now.'

Speaking more about the lengths Mayniacs and their mums go to, he told MTV in a 2013 interview: 'I went to a club for my birthday with all my friends and this woman had her phone out, she was filming everything, and we were a bit like, "What is she doing?" so I went up to her and said, "Can I help you?" she said, "oh uh," and she got out this text and her daughter had sent her a text saying, "It's Conor Maynard's birthday, he's gonna be in this club tonight can you please go and meet him."

'So her mum came to this club alone, all dressed up, just to say, "My daughter loves you", and I was like, "Thanks... you can go now!" haha and then she left! I remember once I was on tour and I was backstage, it was kind of like on the second floor so the fans created a human ladder outside of the wall to climb through the window to kind of try and touch me.'

He added: 'I didn't know what they were trying to do! But I just put my hand through the window and was like, "Please, please!" so we had to shut the window and tell them not to do that because it was dangerous.'

It seems Conor has everything that he could have wanted. He said: 'Everything that has happened so far has been amazing, but I'm not about to take my eye off the ball. Right now I'm getting ready for the next step because I don't want to trip myself up. This is the most exciting thing to happen to me, and I don't want it to stop.'

However, he couldn't have completed this incredible journey by himself. There are few artists who have such a close relationship with the fans. His musical adventure all began with a fan base, and not because of heavy-handed promotion and manufactured hype. It all started with a boy putting up songs on the internet and fans falling in love with his efforts. There is something genuine about Conor's relationship with his fans – they made him and he seems eager to ensure they share his journey with him.

Or, as he aptly put it on Twitter: 'Me and #Mayniacs are gettin' married to fame, And all you bitches that be hatin' can catch the bouquet.'

DISCOGRAPHY

UK

SINGLES
Can't Say No
Released April 2012
U.K. Peak Position – Number 2

Vegas Girl
Released July 2012
U.K. Peak Position – Number 4

Turn Around
Feat. Ne-Yo

Released October 2012
U.K. Peak Position – Number 8

Animal
Feat. Wiley
Released January 2013
U.K. Peak Position – Number 6

ALBUM
Contrast
Released July 2012
U.K. Peak Position – Number 1
Animal/Turn Around/Vegas Girl/Can't Say No/Lift Off/Mary Go Round/Take Off/Better Than You/Another One/Pictures/Glass Girl/Just In Case.